Relish

HOW TO FEED YOUR FRIENDS

WITH

Relish

JOANNA WEINBERG

BLOOMSBURY

To Ed, the first to ask for more.

First published in Great Britain in 2007

Text © 2007 by Joanna Weinberg
Photography © 2007 by Francesca Yorke
Illustrations © 2007 by Clementine Hope

The moral right of the author has been asserted.

Bloomsbury Publishing Plc, 36 Soho Square, London W1D 3QY

A CIP catalogue record for this book is available from the British Library.

ISBN 9780747583448

10 9 8 7 6 5 4 3 2 1

Designer: Georgia Vaux
Photographer: Francesca Yorke
Illustrator: Clementine Hope/NB Illustration

Quotation on page 5 from Helen Fielding's *Bridget Jones's Diary* is reproduced by kind permission of Picador, Pan Macmillan. Recipe on page 72 for Yoghurt cake with pistachios from *The Moro Cookbook*, published by Ebury Publishing, is reproduced by kind permission of The Random House Group Ltd.

Printed in Great Britain by Butler and Tanner Ltd, Frome.

FSC

Mixed Sources

Product group from well-managed
forests and other controlled sources

Cert no. SA-COC-1654 AG
www.fsc.org
© 1996 Forest Stewardship Council

Mark Darcy seemed very pleased when I rang him up. 'What are you going to cook?' he said. 'Are you good at cooking?'

'Oh, you know . . .' I said. 'Actually I usually use Marco Pierre White. It's amazing how simple it can be if one goes for a concentration of taste.'

He laughed and then said, 'Well, don't do anything too complicated. Remember everyone's coming to see *you*, not to eat parfaits in sugar cages.'

Bridget Jones's Diary

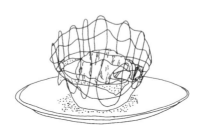

CONTENTS

INTRODUCTION

This is a book about food and friendship, and cooking and love. It is not exactly a cookbook, though it contains lots of recipes, nor is it a domestic manual, though it does have ideas for home and kitchen in it. It's not a rulebook for the socially anxious, either; in fact it dispenses with etiquette entirely – manners may be important, but ideas about what is 'proper' and 'correct' are outdated. It is meant for anyone who loves food and loves people, and believes that where the two meet, a kind of alchemy occurs.

In order to tell you where it began, come back for a minute to 1992. John Major is re-elected as Prime Minister. The poll tax is abolished. London is in love with sun-dried tomatoes but no one's yet heard of Jamie Oliver. In the northeast, the Stadium of Light is still called Roker Park, the best night out in Newcastle is gay night at Rockshots, and I'm at college in Durham.

It's here that I was first hit by the cooking bug, and it was my sister Sam's fault. She's six years older than me, and while I was enduring institutional food, she was living it up in London, eating out at restaurants and discovering extra-virgin olive oil. She also had a place of her own, which had a narrow spindly table that could more or less fit six people round it (that is, as long as their legs weren't very long).

She made jewel-coloured risottos that she served with hunks of fresh Parmesan to grate at the table, and warm chicken salads in the summer with dressings made from crème fraîche and fresh tarragon. She peeled cucumber and fried sage, roasted butternut and baked plums. And every day, just after *Neighbours*, she'd call me up and I'd drool as she whispered reports of her food life down the wire. People thought we were pretty weird to run our relationship more or less solely on the topic of food, and maybe we were.

I wanted to join the food revolution, too. Admittedly, the options on next to no budget in the Northeast at the time were limited. There was a Safeways with a poorly selection of oils, a variety of frozen oven-cooked chips and a lot of woolly apples. But there were good local eggs and vegetables at the Saturday market in the main square, and when I moved out of halls into an old miner's cottage with friends, there, in the middle of our freezing galley kitchen with pebbledash walls and a wobbly Formica table, was an oven to be used any time I so desired.

And I did – hesitantly at first and then with increasing confidence. I practised with garlicky frittata and spinach risotto, spaghetti with lemon, homemade pesto, then ragù. People came and sat round the table and we got through a lot of Bulgarian Cabernet Sauvignon. On weekends at home, I'd beg recipes from my stepmother and pinch her old linen tea towels to take back with me.

But the great romance was between me and my cookbooks. I wanted to spend any spare money seeking out decent ingredients, and time transforming them. I wanted to chop and simmer and stew. I spurned Delia for not being sexy enough, and embraced Nigel (like a movie star, he needs no surname) with a passion he would find shocking. I took him to bed and read him huddled under the duvet throughout the bleak winter. Since pancetta and fresh Parmesan were hard to come by, often the meals I made remained fantasies, but my dreams were filled with happy, noisy people sitting around a table, stuffing their faces.

I began to read cookbooks with an eye to what was realistic in terms of my own life – as soon as they used the words 'whiz in the processor', or 'fresh truffles', I turned the page. I developed a loathing for intricate cooking that couldn't be prepared in advance, or that could go wrong – curdle, burn, etc. – at the last minute. I wanted to know which recipes used the least kit and caused the least mess.

Having people over was my way of saying, hi, I like you, please will you be in my life. Gradually, I became aware that cooking was about people even more than it was about food. I became frustrated if recipes didn't take into account the context in which I was cooking; many of them spoke to me as if money was no object and inviting people round was about impressing them, not spending time with them. In their enticing descriptions of asparagus glossy with hollandaise, or pan-fried scallops with balsamic mash, they failed to point out that I needed to be standing over the stove for the final 45 minutes, stirring a boiling pot that would melt any make-up I'd attempted, or need to be dished up individually so that I never got to sit down until the first person's food was cold.

So what is this book about? Well, it's about all the different elements that contribute to a great evening at home with friends. It may be that there are times when a wine box and a shoulder to cry on are more appreciated than a slow roast shoulder of lamb, and others when all you want to do is celebrate with a place full of flowers and huge cake; I've included both. There are sensible ideas for coping with small spaces (great one-pot dinners and half-made, half-bought carpet picnics), as well as simple tricks to make an evening feel grand (wine decanted into a jug, lots of candlelight and long-stemmed white lilies).

I've tried hard not to be too prescriptive. But from time to time, when I feel strongly that a particular trick will really make your life easier – like ditching starters – I can get quite pedantic (I haven't included recipes for starters at all, only 'bits' for people to pick at while they're waiting). Ignore me, of course, if my ideas don't suit you. But know this: I would no more fuss with complicated napkin arrangements than take up golf, nor have I ever been interested in frilly food.

I'm not going to try to convince you to 'entertain' more often. What I want to do is encourage you through different situations – both social and culinary – that you'll encounter along the way. Do what you do, however you like to do it; have confidence in it, and there's nothing that can be 'wrong'. In the end, food is love; at least it is to me. That's all, really. To me, that's everything.

Cast of characters

SAM, my older sister, is a country mum with an impractical penchant for pencil skirts and red stilettos. She's responsible for my love of cooking, infecting me with an enthusiasm in my late teens that turned into a roll around my middle which took a very broken heart to shed. We've spent a disproportionate amount of time together talking about food. She also shares my passion for the home section of weekend supplements and shopping (window, of course), though her obsession with detective fiction leaves me cold.

KATE, my little sister, is cloaked in glamour. She never wears socks, rarely carries cash and is word perfect in all twelve episodes of *Fawlty Towers*. She's a great guest when she's not stuck in the car pound trying to charm the release of her beaten-up Mini. Not only does she turn up, armed with flowers and wine in exactly the right gear for any occasion, she actually hones her anecdotes for optimum entertainment.

ED is my boyfriend. He's built like the BFG, with a heart as big as a house and consumes food accordingly, guzzling snozzcumbers whole and swishing them down with pint-sized gulps of red wine. Sam set us up over a dinner she cooked (long-marinated steak, samphire, many many bottles of wine), and that was that, really. Brilliant at making friends and chat in general, he is committed to games, particularly those he can win.

Walk-on parts are awarded to Sam's husband **MARK** and their two kids, **ALFIE** and **NOTTY** because they always let me stay in the much-fought-over spare room for their summer party. Also, my designer stepmother **NOUSH** from whom I have learnt by osmosis to feel my way to style, and my **DAD**, who never knows where any of his kids are (there are six of us), but is, nevertheless, a doll, and excellent at blackened pepper steaks, overdone roast potatoes and midnight feasts of Matzos and Marmite.

My friends, who tend not to be too unlike me, only a bit better, include: **DAISY**, who looks like Marilyn Monroe, cooks like an angel and laughs like a drain; and **MIN** who grew up with me, though she wore jeans and hippy beads while I was in knickerbockers and frilly socks.

And **ME?** I'm a cheese/chocolate/red wine kind of girl. I was never particularly aware of this until I spent several years living in America with plastic cheese, 'chocolate' that may as well have been sugary mud, and red wine so treacly you'd still be sucking it off your teeth the next day. I'm the person who won't ever leave the kitchen whether it's a party or a telly supper. I love fiddling around in it. I even love cleaning it. I don't know where it comes from particularly, but all I can say is that having lived in New York for a couple of years without one (truly, kitchen-free apartments exist there), you practically have to attach a ring to my nose and drag me away from mine since I moved back.

A note about the food, and in particular, roast chicken

I love reading recipes. To me they tell stories of happy evenings, perfect-length fairytales to read at bedtime before my eyelids droop. I have been inspired by so many loved and trusted books, magazines and friends over the years that I can no longer trace the origins of many of my recipes. They are as likely to have started life between the pages of an ancient Constance Spry as a column in the Sunday papers. This book is therefore a 'best of' the recipes that I regularly use.

Each menu comes as an idea for which situation it might best work in, according to season, practicality, cost and numbers. Some contain several recipes; often I will point you in the direction of the deli counter or patisserie. I have tried to get a realistic balance, which will hopefully mean these meals are all within reach despite the time constraints of a working life. They are just suggestions, but the timing and balance of each should work for the situation for which it is intended. Of course, you can switch them around. But bear in mind that some dishes bring with them natural economies of scale – both in terms of expense and time. For example, although Manuela's chicken and tarragon pie (page 147) could make a romantic supper for two, it would be just the same amount of work as it would have been for six, so why not choose something like the baked bream on page 205 instead? It's a natural-sized portion for a cosy supper in, and less work, too.

One of the problems with the idea of cooking for friends is that it often becomes 'entertaining'. People get stuck thinking they have to turn a friendly supper into a dinner party, building a meal from impressive (and costly) ingredients, which they then have to do something complicated with. As a guest, while it's heart-warming to know that your host has spent time and energy cooking for you, it's stressful to be aware that they've spent a small fortune doing it.

When the occasion is important or large, don't go for restaurant-style food that needs serving individually. It's a much more stressful way of cooking. Instead, invert expectations and give yourself a break by attaching a simple, earthy dish that can be made in advance (which often improves it) like pie or stew. A table full of people who don't know each other will be bound by a shared dish of rustic food, which is welcome in any situation. Instead, save delicate cooking and expensive ingredients – like spatchcocked quail or rack of lamb – for a small number who will really appreciate them.

About starters: I don't make them. But you'll see that some menus have a recipe for a dish – often some kind of dip – that could function either as a starter or for people to eat while they're standing around. I hope these recipes will become friends that will relieve you of the anxious pauses that starters often cause while you disappear to finish off the main course. They're randomly spread throughout the menus, but should work in any context. They are optional, though, and can always be replaced with a plate of olives and salami.

And finally, a plea from the heart: when you're too busy and life overwhelms you, don't give up cooking for friends. Nourishing others will, in return, nourish you: it tends to put things back into perspective. You can fall back on roast chicken: it's as straightforward as cooking gets, and I can think of no one who doesn't love eating roast chicken with good fresh bread and lots of salad to mop up the gravy. Remember, it's the people that are important.

My favourite roast chicken

- 1 head garlic or 1 small onion, peeled
- 1 medium-sized free-range chicken
- small bunch of thyme or other fresh herbs
- 1 lemon
- olive oil
- 1 large glass white wine
- salt and black pepper

Heat the oven to 220°C/gas 7. Slice off the top of the garlic head so that the cloves are exposed, and push the whole head (or the onion) into the cavity of the chicken, along with half the thyme. Cut the lemon in half, squeeze a little of the juice over the chicken and into the cavity. Push both halves of the lemon into the cavity cut-side first – the second one will stick out but no matter. Rub the skin all over with olive oil. Scatter over the rest of the herbs and be very generous with salt and fresh black pepper.

Put the chicken in a roasting tin, add the glass of wine along with a glass of water (this will turn into perfect gravy) and roast for 15 minutes. Baste the bird, then turn down to 190°C/gas 5 and roast for a further 45 minutes. Check the juices by pulling the leg joint and piercing the inner thigh with the tip of a pointed knife: if they're still running pink, return to the oven for 5 to 10 minutes. When done, let rest for at least 10 forgiving minutes before carving. Skim the surplus fat off the pan juices, and serve alongside the chicken.

1. THE SECRET IS TO BE PREPARED

Planning any occasion can be the most daunting part of it. Even if you only have a couple of cookbooks, you'll still be confronted with an overwhelming amount of choice, and while it's appealingly safe to fall back on old favourites, trying something new can bring a certain freshness to the occasion. So where, and how, to start?

It's tempting to get overwhelmed by food fashion, which seems to change as quickly as skirt shapes and sleeve lengths. As with clothes, much better to find your own style. What you feel like eating will be what you'll cook best. This could vary, depending on your mood or the weather. Sometimes it will be the stews, pies and orchard fruits of home, on other occasions you will be steered towards the sweet tomatoes, cured meats and aromatic herbs of the Mediterranean, or the fragrant curries and coconut broths of the East.

Put convention aside to think about what sort of dishes suit your cooking – as often as not, it's a process of elimination. Are you best at concentrating on getting the flavours right in one central dish, or would you feel less stressed by a series of smaller tapas-style plates where it wouldn't matter if one went wrong? Taking into account what you have in terms of kit, and whether you want to invest in more will take you to the next step.

Much may depend on what is easily available to you – with foresight, you may be able to order it all in advance but as often as not, you'll be reaching for last-minute local support from delis, butchers and other food specialists, and that will also shape your plans.

Finally – though they should possibly come at the top of this list – your guests: who is coming? What sort of people are they – formal or relaxed, traditional or laid back? Knowing them, in combination with the type of occasion it is, will help you nail down the ideal menu.

If you get in a state about it, try conjuring up an image of the meal in full swing instead – it's my equivalent of breathing into a paper bag to calm down. You'll see immediately that no one will notice you forgot the bread, or the parsley, or if you're a tiny bit short of rice.

Like packing to go on holiday, you'll most likely try to fit in too much. Dream up the perfect menu, and then ditch a course. While you may not always want to simplify a meal (some evenings call for bells and whistles), below are some ideas for when you do:

First rule of simplification: *Ditch Your Starter*

Starters are hell for a host with no help and little time. They bring with them a full sink, dirty cutlery, the clattering interruption of plates being cleared and a noticeable absence of the host who is sweating over the main course.

Much of the fuss and anxiety of making an evening run smoothly disappears along with the starter. Have instead some bits like olives and charcuterie for people to pick at when they arrive. You can add to the bought ones by making something extra like a Middle Eastern dip or salad if you have time. You can bank on the first few guests wanting to hang out with you in the kitchen while you're finishing up the rest of the preparations – as with parties, people are immediately drawn into its comforting warmth and noise. If you feel really strongly about three courses, buy one or two cheeses to eat with salad after the main course (off the same plate, like the French, saves on washing up).

Second rule of simplification: *Assemble your pudding*

The world is divided into people who believe there's no point in cooking unless you make pudding, and those who are just as happy with cheese or chocolate. But there's a third way: so many delicious puddings can be assembled simply from two or three ingredients without the need to switch on the oven. I'm not saying don't make – or bake – puddings ever, but save it for when you have time. Otherwise, a beautiful tart from the patisserie will always please, but when you're stuck, anything sweet will do: a couple of bars of chocolate broken into shards, or bought 'homemade' brownies or chocolate biscuit cake cut into bite-sized pieces and piled onto a plate. A big bowl of one type of fruit looks more elegant than a mixed bowl of fruit; cherries, lychees, grapes or anything that people can eat straight from the bowl with their fingers will make your life easier. And finally, all of Gü's ready-made chocolate puddings are terrific.

Third rule of simplification: *Salad Goes With Everything*

It's the best stop-gap ever, and however much you meant to braise the fennel or do something interesting with beans, you might get stuck working late, or just run out of steam. Somehow salad works as well to mop up the gravy of a winter roast as it does to cleanse your mouth after a sticky paella. It doesn't have to be the same salad each time. Different leaves go with different tastes, and you can add all sorts of other seasonal bits too – tiny raw asparagus tips in the spring, fresh peas in the summer, avocado whenever you can lay your hands on a ripe one. I generally bring it out with the main course and leave it on the table – some people like to have it at the same time, others prefer to eat it afterwards.

All families have a resident dressing-maker, and in mine, it's me: I take one one part walnut oil and one part olive oil (you can just use olive if you don't have walnut but, long-term, it's worth the investment) and one part lemon juice. I like to add more Dijon mustard than one might instinctively (per two parts of oil, you'll need just under one part of mustard), a really good scramble of salt and pepper, and beat with a fork. Enough mustard and it will emulsify into a creamy thickness. Taste to check the seasoning before tossing really thoroughly with the salad just before serving.

I digress. So the main course is all you have left to think about, in terms of proper cooking. First think about what you feel like eating. What haven't you eaten for ages? What's the weather like? What's in season? Are you more comfortable with stovetop cooking or using the oven? If you are looking up recipes, concentrate on dishes that can be cooked in one pot or tin. They tend to be more straightforward: roasts are particularly good for this, as are pies and stews. No one wants a host who is going to spend the evening playing martyr in the kitchen. It sounds obvious, but your guests are your friends and they have come to spend time with you, as well as eat your food.

Finding the perfect flavour fit

There are some ingredients that perfectly bring out the flavour in others. It's often down to a geographical partnership: from the Med come basil, tomatoes, garlic and olive oil; lamb, chickpeas, feta and saffron from the Middle East; coconut, lemongrass, chilli and coriander from the Far East. It's incredibly useful to have these to hand or in your head when you're figuring out what you want to make – or when you're shopping, and suddenly go for a change in direction. (In fact, you may be surprised at how many you instinctively know.) The suggestions below are shamelessly adapted from Nigel Slater's handy list in *Appetite*.

Anchovy: potatoes, black olives, lamb
Basil: tomatoes, mozzarella
Bay: beef, stocks
Black pepper: salads, strawberries, almost everything apart from saffron and truffles
Capers: lamb, most fish, anchovy
Cardamom: cream, lamb, chocolate, coffee, rice
Cinnamon: lamb, apples
Coffee: dark chocolate, walnuts
Coriander: avocado, chicken, lentils, chickpeas
Cumin: lamb, pumpkins and squash, potatoes
Garlic: lamb, chicken, fish, aubergines, mushrooms, tomatoes, etc., into infinity
Lemon: chicken, pork, all fish
Mint: lamb, potatoes, peas
Mustard: pork, beef
Nutmeg: milk, potatoes
Orange: chocolate, rhubarb
Rosemary: lamb, beef, anything barbecued
Saffron: most fish, chicken, rice
Sage: pork, butter
Soy sauce: pork, greens, avocado, rice
Tarragon: chicken, white fish
Thyme: red meat, pumpkins and squash, in fact anything roasted

Food friends

Some foods seem to exist so perfectly together they could almost be married. Again, apologies and thanks to Nigel Slater.

Steak and peppery salad leaves
Chicken and leeks
Fish and fennel
Mozzarella and olive oil
Blue cheese, walnuts and frisée
Cheese and good jam or chutney
Cheese and red wine
Parma ham and figs
Charcuterie and cornichons
Lamb, houmous and pine nuts
Asparagus and Parmesan
Artichokes and butter
Chocolate, coffee, booze
Berries, cream and pastry

Planning ahead, particularly if you're by yourself

(Oh, and by the way, this is not particularly pointed at single people, because unless you're lucky, partners in the kitchen are generally about as helpful as loose marbles rolling around the floor.)

If you know you're not going to have much help, try and think ahead a bit. I know it's not always possible, but in a perfect world remembering to buy candles whenever you are at the supermarket rather than on the day, or flowers a day ahead (which will also give them a chance to open up) will go a long way to helping you feel prepared.

Look for recipes that you can cook, at least in part, in advance; this is the time to produce that pie you made earlier. Otherwise, buy-in part of the meal from supermarket, deli or butcher – as I've said before, there's nothing wrong with feeding people something pre-prepared as long as you have put some real love into one part of the evening. It may be a homemade mayonnaise (good for upper arm tone), a terrific pudding (less good for any muscle tone) or making the table

look very pretty. Stay away from pasta or risotto (unless there are five or less of you) – both involve last-minute stress and a steam-facial. And don't be afraid to ask any of your guests to pick up something you've forgotten on their way.

Some thoughts about wine, and its accompanying 'laws'

I've always been wary of wine rules. Not because I don't believe they work – I'm sure they do. It's more that, in all honesty, the wine most of us drink most of the time is not good enough to significantly enhance what we're eating or vice versa. What we drink is more likely to be influenced by the time of day and the weather – when it's hot we want cold and light, when it's cold we want richer and warming. Likewise in the day people are drawn towards the lightness of white, whereas the night brings longings to be sunk by big reds.

But if you're interested in the rules, keep in mind that generally white comes before red, and light before heavy; that pale food tends to be accompanied by white wine, and rich, dark food, by red. Rosé allows you to sit on the fence. My only advice is to drink the best bottle you have first and follow with the plonk as you'll care less and less what it tastes like as the night goes on. For general defining characteristics and extremely loose guidelines, see page 277.

PS. A note for guests

About whether to bring wine: in general, if you're going to dinner at a friend's house, turn up with a bottle of wine as an offering – they may be counting on it. Bring whichever colour you'd like to drink, or call in advance and ask what they'd prefer. If, however, you're going to dinner with people older, grander, or significantly richer and more stylish than you, don't – they may feel obliged to open it out of politeness, and it could be less good than what they'd planned to serve. In this case, a bunch of flowers or a box of unusual chocolates or sweetmeats are a better bet.

Kitting yourself out

While cookbooks sometimes give the impression that you can't start boiling an egg unless you own a limitless *batterie de cuisine*, in terms of space and cost it makes more sense to acquire kitchenware piecemeal. Unless you're getting married – the ultimate one-stop shopping opportunity – it builds up over time, and brings with it memories and attachments which are more important (to me at least) than matching sets.

You can go far on a couple of good knives, a few pans, a sieve and a wooden spoon. Against my instincts, I invested in a food processor for the first time earlier this year. It takes me ages to figure out how to use it each time, washing it up bothers me, and the amount of space it takes up compared to the frequency with which I use it doesn't pay off. Perhaps one day it will, but for the time being I get cross every time the kettle bumps into it. I have tried to avoid too many recipes in this book for which you really need a whizzer, as I've always managed without one. A friend once bought me a very sharp, orange plastic mandolin at a market in France; it's effective and fast. Chopping by hand (like making sauces and pastry if you've got the time) can be therapeutic; if there's more than one of you it's not so slow, either. Over time you'll find the perfect mixing bowl and a couple of serving dishes, but you never need as much as a shiny kitchen shop will entice you to buy. It's worth poking through oriental supermarkets whenever you come across one – they sell amazing knives, pretty multi-purpose bowls, and cheap bamboo steamers: all worth their weight in gold.

In terms of serving and eating, I don't believe you have to have full sets of anything. All you really need in the end are enough plates to eat off, glasses to drink from, and knives and forks to eat with.

I do, nevertheless, rely on a few kitchen 'stars' that make a big difference:

• Wooden boards of all shapes and sizes: not only are they essential for chopping, but great to serve general nibbles on, and cheese too. Any piece of reclaimed wood will do for serving, unusual shapes and sizes make a plain table look more interesting and original. Give it a good scrub and after that it should only need oiling from time to time to prevent it splitting.

• Resealable plastic bags: these are my guilty secret. If I had to write a eulogy for a single piece of kitchen equipment, it would be for these environmentally unfriendly godsends. I have them in all different sizes: for marinating meat, crushing biscuits, freezing bread, stock and grated cheese, for picnics and storing almost anything that is lurking in the fridge.

• Small bowls, dishes and jugs: these are great for lots of things – butter, olives and nuts, ashtrays, separating eggs, making dressings, serving mustard, mayonnaise, ketchup, milk and cream, decorating the table. Keep an eye out when you pass charity and junk shops, and markets. What could look twee as part of a set might be pretty on its own.

• Tea towels: I like the old-fashioned ones with a single stripe of colour through them. As well as being useful dishcloths, they are great as tablecloths, tea cosies, on trays, and for disguising ugly pots and pans. Ironed well, they make huge napkins, too, which you can spread over your lap like a tablecloth just for you.

Stocking the larder

If I were to wave my wand and have the perfect larder that (apart from a few fresh ingredients on top) would enable me to be ready to cater for any situation, the ingredients below are what I'd have to hand. If the list seems daunting, remember it is my fantasy list. Like kit, ingredients will accrue over time, as and when you need them.

Freezer

Good Parmesan – either in a block or grated

Lean mince – for bolognese, meatballs, cottage pie

Fresh chicken stock

A whole chicken

Peas – can either be a veg, an immediate soup (with the stock and Parmesan), or go into a salad

Spinach, leaf if possible – side dish, soup, fried up with chilli and lemon for pasta, a stuffing for flatbread, or the perfect risotto (with the stock and Parmesan again)

Prawns – preferably ethical cold-water ones from the North Atlantic

Bread – a good loaf, sliced by me and kept in a plastic bag for toast

Wine – leftover glasses of wine can be frozen to use in cooking

Berries – don't defrost well, but great eaten with hot white chocolate sauce, cooked into any pie or compote, or blended with yoghurt as a smoothie

Preparation

Fridge

Butter
Milk
Eggs
Good Parmesan – in a block
Pancetta
Salami or cured ham
Salad leaves
Fresh herbs
Carrots
Celery
Dijon mustard
Pomegranate molasses
Homemade pesto
Beer
White wine
A bottle of fizz

Herbs, spices and sugars

Sea salt
Black peppercorns
Cardamom
Cumin seeds
Coriander seeds
Ground ginger
Dried chilli
Whole nutmeg
Cinnamon
Dried oregano
Smoked paprika, hot or sweet
Vanilla extract and pods
Dark muscovado sugar
Raw caster sugar
Fructose

Store cupboard

Pasta
Risotto rice
Paella rice
Basmati rice
Strong bread flour
Plain white flour
Olive oil
Walnut oil
Tinned tomatoes
Tinned chickpeas
Tinned flageolet or cannellini beans
Puy lentils
Tahini
Peanut butter
Pine nuts
Sunflower and pumpkin seeds
Soy sauce
Worcestershire sauce
Japanese pickled ginger
Nam pla (Thai fish sauce)
Ketchup
Red wine
Baking potatoes
Onions
Garlic
Lemons
Fresh ginger
Rosewater
Orange-flower water
Blanched almonds
Good chocolate

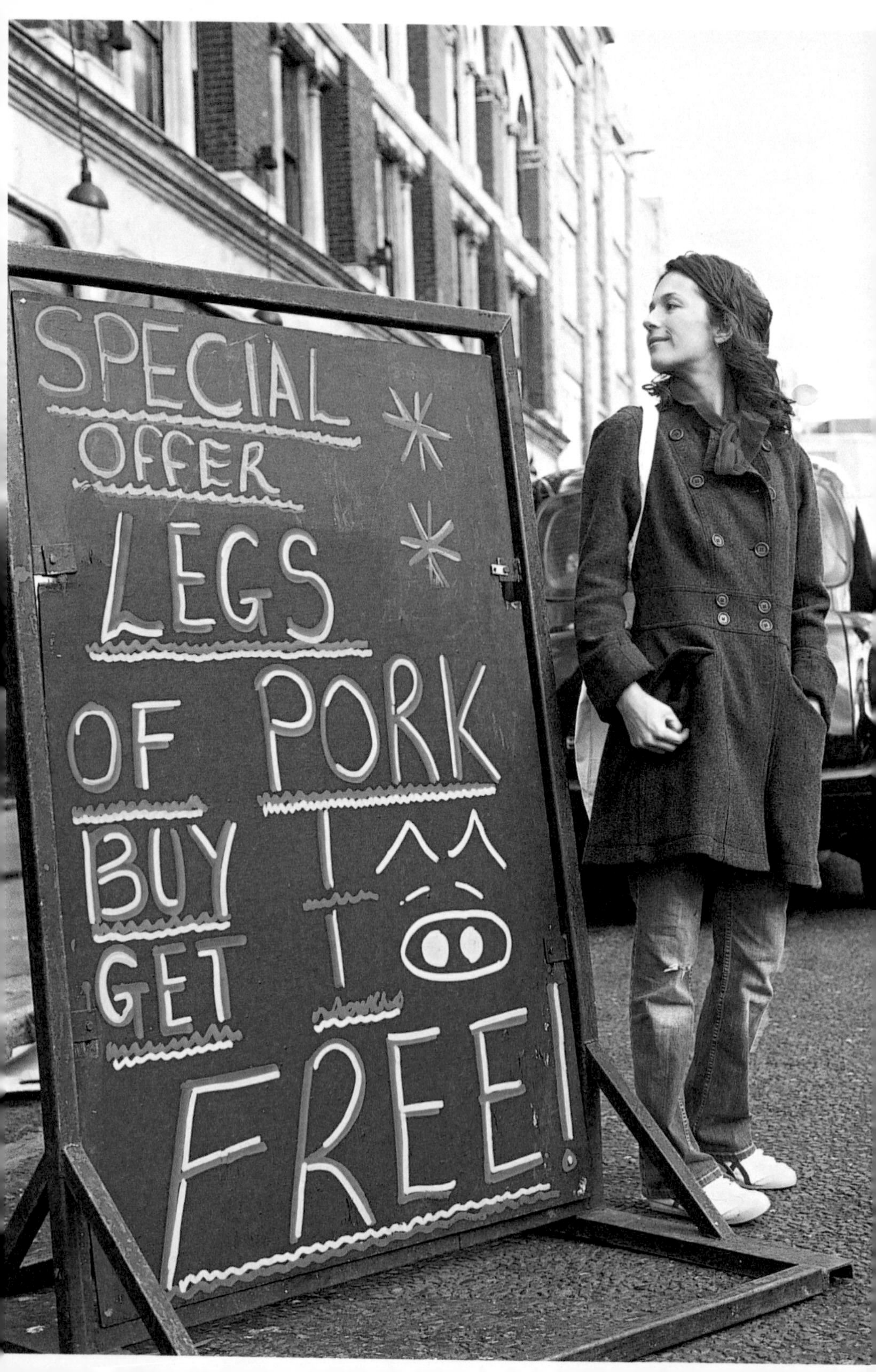
SPECIAL
OFFER
LEGS
OF PORK
BUY 1
GET 1
FREE!

Preparation

Some thoughts on shopping, including a plea to stay local

What a treat, shopping to please other people. Making an evening feel special can be as much about clever shopping as about elaborate cooking. Most of us have access to farmers' markets and/or local independent food sellers who really know their stuff. Support them when you can. They are the guardians of quality and will be founts of knowledge about buying clever cuts of meat, seasonal produce and other ways to enjoy the best without having to be profligate.

I find myself magnetically drawn to delis for bowls of glossy olives, haunches of cured hams begging to be sliced by the handsome Italian boy, or a beautifully packaged bar of chocolate. When guests are coming over, I treat myself with a visit to my favourite independent specialists to pick up the huge paper bag of cherries and a whole runny cheese that I can never justify for myself.

I beg you not to do the heavy stuff (vegetables, drinks) on the same day as your dinner. For a start, you spare yourself the Panic of the Missing Ingredient. But even if everything's available, going for a frantic expedition will mean that by the time you've got home and unpacked it all, you are not going to feel like picking up a knife to start chopping.

Boring but important

Changing shopping habits makes a huge difference to our environment. Supermarkets really are squeezing small producers and the quality, variety and flavour is disappearing from our food and our high streets. Support specialist shops whenever you can. Obviously, it is a bit more expensive, but as with anything, there are sensible choices you can make that collectively affect small-holding farmers, food production in general, and finally, the ingredients on your plate:

• Buy seasonally. Gluts of produce will always drive the price down in grocers and markets, but in supermarkets too.
• Buy locally. Cut down on the miles your food travels. You'll be supporting local producers as well as lowering carbon emissions. Don't be duped into thinking organic food is always better for the environment: it could easily be coming from the other side of the world, so check the label.
• Buy from specialists. Butchers and fishmongers should know where food has come from and how it's been treated and caught.

• For meat, spend the same money but buy cheaper cuts of good meat, rather than fancier cuts of cheap produce. (The only meat I'd beware of here is lamb – the cheapest cuts, like neck, can be very fatty indeed).

• For fish, to support stock levels, seek out fish that has been line, creel or diver caught, and avoid anything that is trawled or dredged. Beware, though, of 'organically farmed' fish – they are mostly fed on pellets made from wild fish; each fish consumes more than its own body weight for every pound it grows. The same goes for prawns, which should be a treat for special occasions only. Buy wild cold water ones, they taste much the best, and are less under threat from over-fishing. Don't bother with farmed warm water tiger prawns – they are ecologically unsound, farmed in polluted conditions, and are watery and tasteless. Check the Marine Conservation Society website (www.fishonline.org) for up-to-date information about species in danger before treating everyone to a giant baked sea bass.

• Don't be shy, ask questions. People power is the only thing that can change supermarket pile-it-high-and-flog-it-cheap attitudes.

The supermarket panic

You've decided what you're going to make. You've simplified it, and figured out whether you've got the right kit. But you've built your whole menu around a particular ingredient that you meant to get yesterday. So you rush to the supermarket on your way home. They don't have it, but the choice is overwhelming. Endless different cuts and grades of pink meat press in on you; glassy-eyed fish, fresh, frozen, smoked, call to you from their icy beds; world-weary vegetables size you up.

Don't panic, it's going to be OK. Keep in mind that there's no such thing as a 'perfect' recipe. You won't need to change the whole dinner just because of a single missing ingredient, even if it's a major one. Think about its colour, texture and the place it takes in the recipe. Try a different cut of the same meat, or even the same cut of a different meat – the butcher will point you in the right direction. Beets and shallots will roast and caramelize as beautifully as carrots and garlic. Watercress has the same peppery spike as rocket.

Mushrooms have a similar meatiness to artichoke hearts. Pecorino substitutes perfectly for Parmesan. Flat-leafed parsley can substitute for almost any herb if needs be.

If you can get your head around trying to imagine the qualities of the ingredients, you'll find that you can fit any recipe around them. A lot of cookery writers seem hell-bent on bankrupting you by sending you out to buy the best, but alternatives often have the bonus of being better value:

On the bench, in case you need them

For:	*Substitute:*
Monkfish	Conger eel
Cod	Pollack
Smoked salmon	Smoked mackerel
Clams	Mussels
Leg of lamb	Shoulder of lamb
Lamb noisettes	Lamb chops
Beef fillet	Pork tenderloin
Veal chop	Pork chop
Artichokes	Mushrooms
Rocket	Watercress
Chard, bok choi	Spinach, greens
Cavolo nero	Kale, spinach
Aubergine	Courgettes
Fennel	Celery
Parmesan	Pecorino

What to do in a shoebox

When I lived in New York, I had a tiny flat that had a cupboard (literally) for a kitchen. It was only then that I realized how important being able to have friends around was to me, so I developed a system for coping without it. It's the only area of my life I've ever executed with military precision. I always made one-pot wonders, doing all the chopping on a board on my knees in front of the telly the night before, so I could concentrate on getting the place in order on the day. Even though I've got more space now, it's a habit that's lingered, and as often as not, when people come around to eat, I'll gravitate towards the suppers that I perfected during that time. If nothing else, they cause a lot less mess.

Small-kitchen tips

You can produce feasts from even the smallest kitchen if you follow these basic methods:

• You'll need all the work surface you can get, so don't leave unnecessary bottles of oil, salt and pepper, tea bags and other kitchen generals lurking on it.

• Get used to the idea that you're not going to be a kit-led cook – there isn't any point in having a food processor/rice cooker/ice-cream maker if you haven't got anywhere to keep it. A couple of good knives and a hand blender do very well, and there's plenty of wonderful food that doesn't involve machinery. Keep an eye out for anything stackable – glasses, mugs, tea-light holders, vases – every inch of space you can buy back will help.

• Have all your ingredients prepared (onions chopped, eggs separated, flour measured, etc.) before you start cooking. This means that you'll be able to tackle one task at a time, and wash and clear up as you go along. I have a series of Ikea bowls that fit snugly into each other for this purpose – as they fill up, I lay them out of harm's way on top of the fridge. If you happen to have a tiffin tin – the old-fashioned stackable containers for picnics – or some stackable Tupperware, this is the job it was born to do.

• If you're determined to do several dishes that need to be ready at once, or more than one course, think carefully about the cooking requirements for each one. You will often find that some kind of salad that can be prepared earlier will work just as well as a hot vegetable. Also, make sure you spread the work between oven and stovetop. Traditions are rooted in practicality, so start new ones that suit you – a joint of meat with vegetables roasted in the juices alongside is just as delicious as doing all the trimmings separately.

• Buy half and prepare half. A curry will still feel homemade if, for example, you buy the dal, rice, and naan, and make the curry, salad and raita yourself.

• Don't get tricked into thinking that canapés (or any individual portions of finger food, like bruschetta) are your solution to anything – they are the most laborious, time and space-consuming food to prepare of all.

Helpful ideas for small living spaces

Tiny living spaces can also be surprisingly easy to reconfigure for guests. It's often just a visual trick to give a feeling of more space – clearing away unnecessary clutter will go a long way to solving space issues. Otherwise, you simply have to be more organized. Here are some possible solutions:

• Clearing surfaces in both the kitchen and living space will allow room for plates/glasses/ashtrays. It's worth seeking out occasional tables that have some kind of storage facility – old trunks make good coffee tables, covered boxes can work very well as side tables.

• Rooms are often arranged around the shrine of the telly, which is not conducive to hanging out with friends, unless television is the point of the gathering. If you can't tuck it away onto a shelf or into a cupboard, consider laying a slightly larger square of chipboard on top of it that you can drape something over, and you've instantly bought yourself an extra table, too.

• A foldaway table. I always thought card tables were very grand until Sam got one on eBay for £20. Not only is it great for after-supper games, she also uses it for civilized telly suppers, romantic dinners for two, and the kids love it for special suppers on their own. It also folds away completely flat and you can store it behind a door.

Supper on the sofa

Sofas are not well designed for eating on and believe me I've tried to find a way around the problem. In the end, I've had to defer to the ancient wisdom of my granny, who has perfected the telly supper. She lays a tray as carefully as she would the table, with mat, napkin, wine glass and a tiny eggcup of flowers. She has a trolley on wheels that she puts it on, along with her food in little dishes (all courses at the same time, like on a plane), and any condiments she needs, and she wheels it over to the sofa. It's a wonderfully comfortable arrangement, and has the added bonus of her being able to put all the dirty stuff back on it, hidden under a tea towel to be forgotten about until the next day.

The trick is really in the tray, not the trolley. Go for the most containable vessel that works. If you're on the sofa, pasta, stews and curries will work best in bowls with a plate underneath to balance, while soups will be happiest in mugs. If you're eating something sloppy, take a couple of tea towels to put across your knees, and over the arm of the sofa, and if you're really messy drape a tablecloth right across you, the sofa and surrounding cushions, so you can slurp with all your heart.

2. SOME THOUGHTS ABOUT SETTING THE SCENE

As a teenager, I'd have put a lot of money against my ever getting into laying the table, fiddling with flowers or thinking about softened light. To me all that stuff conjured up the formality and fuss that never belonged in my idea of a home. But I've come to realize that making your home soft and welcoming is a signal to your guests that you are expecting them, and looking forward to it. So I've grown to appreciate the small delights of the so-called feminine touch. Make it as simple as you like, and keep in mind that all you are doing is creating a small world that is friendly, safe and comfortable, and just a little special.

Laying the table

If the kitchen is the heart of the house, the table is its soul. It's where you sit in the morning when the day is full of promise, and at night when you're spent. It's a place to commune over a candle and a bottle of red as well as disappear into solitary daydreams over the Sunday papers. It's where you chop out your love into onions for soup, and decorate cakes for tea. It should be a place full of romance, imagination and delight. It's not surprising that at the auction of Elizabeth David's things after her death, it was her kitchen table that Prue Leith bought.

More often than not, the kitchen/dining table becomes a central dumping ground, as likely to be used for doing admin and leaving notes for the rest of the household as for eating. When you're having people round, you first need to sweep the mess of life off it and out of your head.

Consider a tablecloth. As you shake it out, the junk of the day goes with it. It doesn't have to be fancy or expensive – you can get a length of plain white cotton (bleached calico is cheapest) from any fabric shop and get your drycleaner to hem the ends. If that seems too formal, try a few large white tea towels, well-pressed. If they cover most of the table or at least the middle of it, you will have a focal point and some sense of ceremony. Mats protect the table as well as framing the plate; a tea towel or large napkin works well for smaller numbers. Best of all, if you're ever passing an oriental supermarket, are the fine bamboo mats used for making sushi rolls. They're cheap and easy to clean and store.

Think of the laid table as a single image rather than lots of different objects, and try to see it in terms of shapes and colours. Food containers – wooden salad bowls, shallow china dishes, a glass fruit bowl – will be decorative in their own right. As a starting point, you've always got the shape of your plates, cutlery and glasses. It doesn't matter whether they match or not. At Sam's summer party each year (see page 175) she lays a trestle table for thirty with a complete mish-mash of plates and bowls, but makes sure that each type is fairly regularly interspersed. The white tablecloth holds the whole thing together, as do jam jars of wild flowers and cow parsley from nearby hedgerows, and tin cans of roses and herbs.

It doesn't have to be flowers though – whatever is in season: bowls of lemons, or stacks of gourds would look just as lovely, as would a more year-round collection of objects, like shells, pebbles or tiny pots of growing herbs.

If you can't fit everything on the table, find another surface nearby for larger objects such as candlesticks, flowers or big bowls – windowsills or side tables work well, and they will still feel part of the same scene. Last time Kate came over for supper, she brought with her a fistful of rosemary and lavender sprigs from her window box and tucked them with some rose petals along the middle of the table between the plates. We put the jug of flowers on the kitchen counter, and the two tall candlesticks on the floor in the corner and it looked pretty and unfussy.

Be wary if all your things crouch very low to the table as the whole room will somehow look flat. This has a tendency to happen with me as I lean towards drinking everything out of tumblers and often use tea lights rather than dinner candles. To avoid this, vary the height of the objects on the table by including a tall jug for water and leaving a couple of opened bottles of wine on the table – or even hang something down from the ceiling. I have several disco balls that hang off ribbons. They started off as a festive addition at Christmas but I never took them down and have grown very attached to them.

If you want a grander feel, find a way of echoing shapes on the table – this could be from matching glasses of different sizes, little dishes for salt and pepper, two or three small jugs for flowers, or for water and wine: as long as something is repeating somewhere – pattern, shape or colour – the table will form a strong, elegant character of its own. Buy long-stemmed white flowers, too. Lilies are your best bet and can even be cost-efficient as they often last a couple of weeks. Light the whole place with candles, loads of them, everywhere: in the hall, up the stairs, in the loo. Use a plain tablecloth and real napkins. And finally, dim your lights very low or switch off any that aren't necessary, in particular overhead ones.

Don't panic if you don't get the table completely done before people arrive. Put something – even if just the plates, glasses and cutlery – on the table as a sign to guests that, unprepared as you are, they are expected and welcome. Someone is bound to turn up before the others and you can always get him or her to pitch in.

A table is not essential to feeding friends; carpet picnics can be just as fun. To feel like you're doing more than just sitting on the floor because you've got no room to do otherwise, invest in a handful of key props. A thick rug is a good start – the floor needs some give. You'll definitely want some large squashy cushions too, though beware beanbags – they're graceless and do no one any favours. If you're arranged around a coffee table, don't use anything too tall – an enormous vase of very tall flowers may look wonderful in the corner of the room but will look plain peculiar if you're staring up at it.

To add a bit of glamour to sitting on the floor, you might want to invest in huge napkins to completely cover your lap like a tablecloth. Old-fashioned tea towels will do the job here, and should be ironed with spray starch for the full effect. Make appropriate food, too. It will feel more natural to eat tapas, Middle Eastern, and/or Asian cooking off the floor, and eating with your hands will work better than trying to cope with something like a roast.

The only difference between a carpet-picnic and a regular picnic is that you have access to an oven, but it's perfectly reasonable to buy in almost everything if that works better for you. Make one of the dishes yourself and choose a warm one, even at the height of summer. The whole meal will feel more homemade and it will tie the rest of the food together.

Florists' tricks for pretty flowers

Choosing flowers, much like laying the table, is very much down to personal style. As with food, if you buy seasonally you are going to get the best value, the happiest blooms, and contribute to your local economy. Any good florist will have ideas about what goes well together and should make up a bunch that looks effective, but should you be faced with a disinterested florist or little choice, here are some helpful thoughts:

• If in doubt, a mass of the one flower in the same colour is infallible and looks generous.

• A mixed-colour bunch of the same flower is generally very cheerful, though it tends to look most balanced if the colours are either all hot or all pastel.

• A mixed bunch in the same tones is also effective.

• If you are only buying a few stems choose longer and more sculptural varieties (iris, lily) that will stand proudly, and the space in between them will become part of the look.

• If you are choosing a mixed bunch, include at least one round-headed flower (gerbera, rose, scabious, chrysanthemum, etc.), as it will hold the whole bunch together visually.

• Choose flowers that look strong and healthy. Leaves and stems should be green and not yellowing. Avoid floppy heads or drooping leaves.

• Strongly scented flowers bring the garden inside. This works magic in a bedroom, bathroom, living room and hall, but can create a Harrods food hall effect in the kitchen/eating area.

• In order that they last as long as possible, pick buds that are just beginning to open but be wary of very tightly closed ones, particularly early in their season, as they may not be mature enough to open at all.

• If you are buying for the same day, avoid flowers in tight bud as they don't have as much impact. But if they are more open, check there is no loose pollen on the petals as this signifies they are coming to the end of their life.

• Consider small shrubs and potted flowers such as lavender, miniature rose and herbs for the table, too. They can be planted into any container, even a milk jug or an old teacup, and will bloom for longer than any cut flower.

How to get the most out of your flowers

Before putting into a vase or bowl, flowers like to be conditioned. To do this:

• Remove leaves below the watermark.

• Cut at least one inch off the stem at a forty-five degree angle as this increases the surface area for water take-up (except hyacinth, tulips and daffodils whose stems can be cut flat across).

• Woody stems also need to be slit so the pith is exposed to the water. Bashing woody stems damages them. Flowers with nodules on the stems, like carnations, should be cut just above the nodule.

• Flowers absorb half the water they need to survive in the first twenty-four hours after being cut. If you have time, let them have a really long drink of tepid water (easier to absorb than cold) and then put them into fresh water in the vase. If you don't, do so the next day. I know this is a bit like being told to floss every night, but your best hope to keep flowers alive as long as possible is to change their water each day. Don't add anything apart from cut flower food to the water.

• To prolong life, trim the stems regularly.

• Remove dead blooms and leaves as they occur. As well as looking sad, they also encourage ageing bacteria to multiply. Avoid standing your flowers too near the fruit bowl for the same reason.

• Avoid leaving them in direct sunlight, heat (beware radiators) or draughts. Flowers keep longest in a cool room, though they won't release as much scent. If they are opening too fast and you are worried about them dying before an event, put them somewhere cool and dark and shut the door in the meantime.

• A bunch of a single type of flower will last longer than a mixed bunch.

The lost art of arranging flowers

Flower-arranging may be one of the lost domestic arts, but it's actually surprisingly easy and quite satisfying, too. Here are the main things you need to keep in mind:

• Consider the setting and context when you're deciding on size – a tiny jug of flowers may get lost in a very large space, but several small jugs can look just as effective and be a more practical and cost-efficient way to use flowers than one grand arrangement.

• Think about whether you want to set off the flowers or the container. Striking-coloured flowers look great in neutral containers, but an ornate vase probably wants a simple bunch.

• Avoid the flowers and the vase being the same volume. The ratio achieves harmony at about 1.5 to one, and it does not matter which is greater in volume, the flowers or their container. Make whichever one you want to focus on the larger.

• With smaller containers, flowers often look better cut short, so the heads just float over the rim.

• Anything that can hold water can be a receptacle for flowers. A used wine or water bottle with a single, sculptural, stem can look as stylish as the smartest vase.

• Tin or enamel buckets and jugs make great informal vases. Beware those with very wide mouths, however, as they may need an awful lot of flowers to make them look good.

Creating a gentle glow

How you use light is surprisingly important, in a background kind of way. Your goal is to create intimacy and atmosphere. Dimming the lights is the obvious place to start; it turns the night on, much in the way that brightening them signifies the end of it. Light that has been diffused – either through a reflection off another surface, or a fairly opaque shade – is the gentlest and most complimentary.

In the living room:

• Go for lots of smaller, lesser light sources rather than a single brighter one. It creates pools of light that people gather into. Table lamps are reassuring and intimate. Use the lowest wattage bulb they can cope with.

• Standard/floor lamps are particularly good in sitting rooms and useful for breaking up rooms where furniture is more or less at the same height.

- Pearl bulbs diffuse light more softly than clear ones.
- Reflecting light diffuses it – point your angle poise towards walls, mirrors and ceilings.
- Putting a plant in front of a lamp will diffuse the light quite well.
- Uplighters are wonderful for a soft, general light, but only work in rooms with fairly high ceilings – if the lamp is too close to the ceiling, it will have a spotlight glare.

Where you eat:

- There's nothing as pretty, flattering and intimate as candlelight. Use whatever shape and size you have or prefer – the more, the merrier. Shot glasses or small tumblers half-filled with sand, soil or salt all make good candlestick impersonators.
- It's important to keep electric light very dim if you have candles and fire, otherwise the flames won't stand out.
- Don't think of fairy lights as a light source but more as a festive addition. The tiny ones look prettiest, whether draped around a window or piled into an empty fireplace or vase. Don't put them on a flashing setting unless you are having a disco.

3. BEHIND THE SCENES

It may seem swotty to plan such things as who sits where, how you're going to dish up the food, and later, to clear the table, but it's this behind-the-scenes stuff that can make an evening run smoothly. It's the sort of forethought that will mean you can concentrate on getting everyone drinks as they arrive, rather than being busted scrabbling in the back of the cupboard for the right dish as the doorbell goes. This hidden work will never be noticed, but the evening will seem to run itself and you can get on with enjoying it.

Who sits where, and why it matters

Doing the seating plan was always Dad's job in our family – there are eight of us altogether so he'd make one even for a family Sunday lunch. Mostly I think he liked to do it because it allowed him to look at us benignly through the spectacles on the end of his nose and make silent assessments of how happy each one of us seemed to be. But because he likes puzzles and has a good memory, each week we'd sit next to a different sibling, and, as we all grew older and moved away, it enabled us to make and retain our individual relationships.

Having people over is sort of like creating a family from scratch. Whether you seat people or just let them fall in will make a big difference to the feel of the evening. There are no rules about whether you do or don't plan it. Until the end of the eighteenth century, people just sat with whom they wished, and only then was the new-fangled idea of 'promiscuous seating' introduced, where men and women were interspersed.

While I used to prefer the spontaneity of an evening that could have been totally different had the jumble emerged – like a childhood game of jacks – in a different pattern, the busier my life gets, the more I've come around to seating plans. Not only does it mean you've paid attention to who might like to talk to each other, but it will also prevent people nervously lurking around the table when you've asked them to sit down. No one likes to sit down first, unless they know where they're supposed to be sitting.

Five is the magic number – less than five, people will all talk together, more and they will break up into different conversations. Of course, a group of old friends will behave differently to a mixed bunch, for whom you will play a more important role. Much depends on the shape of your table. Mine is long and thin, and I have a bench rather than chairs along one side, which means that people find it easier to talk to the person opposite them than their neighbour. A round or square table means the opposite. Treat it like a puzzle – draw a map of your table with marks where all the chairs are and then fill them in with the names on Post-its so you can move them around until they slot into place.

If there are people you particularly want to meet each other, make sure that they are within talking distance. First and foremost, though, look after yourself – if you're not having fun, it will be hard for anyone else to. Often there's someone you'd particularly like to talk to, so make sure that they're next to you. I never mind what the balance of men to women is and quite often I'd rather sit next to a friend than her boyfriend. Don't feel plagued by convention – the man/woman placement only came about in Victorian times because women were thought too dainty to look after themselves.

Mark's card trick

Sometimes pot-luck is the best way of seating people, particularly for large numbers where a plan becomes more sweat than it's worth. This is one solution, but it's a bit complicated to explain; you may need to read this twice, but it's worth following as it is an inspired way to manage lots of people. Here goes: in order to make this work, you need two packs of cards. If, for example, you have sixteen people coming, ten women and six men, take the same ten cards in red (for the girls) from both packs, and the same six cards in black (for the men) from both packs. Lay one card by each place in the configuration of your choice – girl/boy/girl, etc. – and then ask your guests to pick a relevantly coloured card (red for girls again) from the other pack at random as they arrive and tell them they will be sitting in whichever place the matching card is at the table.

Now you have a seating plan without having had to go to the effort and responsibility of making one. Everyone will have fun working out where they're sitting and who they're sitting next to, rather than hanging around like lost sheep waiting to be told. By the way, make sure you hold on to the card belonging to the place where you want to sit; that way you can fix who you want to sit next to by swapping the cards around on the table.

A cautionary tale

Recently, I had some people around for a dinner that went wrong because of people sitting in the wrong place. These were the people involved:
* Me: obviously
* Ed: who thinks media people are up themselves
* Cath: one of my best friends, who works at a newspaper and is still getting to know Ed
* Jerry: her fiancé, a friendly, silent type who suddenly finds his voice in a bottle of wine
* Darren: a good friend of Cath's from work, single, who I wanted to introduce to Daisy

- Daisy: another of my best friends, single, fabulous but sometimes shy
- Rose: Daisy's sister, an opinionated writer who wanted to pitch a story to Darren's paper

I didn't have time to make a seating plan and this is how it turned out:

Jerry	Rose	Ed
Daisy	Darren	Cath	Me

My mistakes:

- Forgetting that people talk across the narrow table more easily than to their neighbours.
- Putting the strongest characters in the middle of the table instead of separating them so conversations could strike up at both ends.
- Seating Daisy and Darren together and separating all the couples, which meant there was no natural rhythm.

What happened:

Darren, being the mystery guest who nobody knew, became the focus. Rose and Ed, who had most access to him, started a noisy debate about the sliding standards of news reporting. This left Daisy and Jerry, who are both a bit shy, stranded. While Jerry is into sport and music, Daisy is more interested in books and films. They struggled. At the other end, Cath and I, though happy to have the time together, couldn't really concentrate because the central conversation dominated everything.

My options:

Change the direction of the conversation. Giving Ed a kick under the table, I could try to engage him, Rose and Cath in a conversation at our end of the table about something innocuous like holiday plans, hoping this would make Darren turn around and pay some attention to Daisy. Jerry, however, would still be a bit stranded.

Or:

I could have moved to the other end of the table after the main course, taking my chair to sit between Jerry and Daisy, which would have given me a bit more control. I could then have started Darren and Daisy in conversation, and talked to Jerry, who I'd like to get to know better, myself. This would have left Ed, Rose and Cath, all confident chatters, to their own devices.

Or:

I could have moved all the men around after the main course. I'm not a big fan of doing this as you have to start all over again just when you get going, but desperate times etc. The better arrangement would have been this:

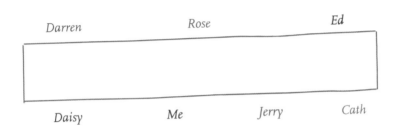

Darren   Rose   Ed

Daisy   Me   Jerry   Cath

Although there is a couple sitting next to each other, because of the shape of the table they would actually have talked across it. Ed could have got to know Cath and Jerry better, Daisy and Darren would have been face to face, with Rose close enough to get involved if they needed help. I could either have saved Daisy and Darren if their conversation was getting sticky, or equally chatted to Jerry and Rose if it was going well.

What I did:

I took the first option, which was the least bold. I felt bad for Jerry, who was left to quietly get drunk by himself at the end of the table. Darren and Daisy did manage to turn in and talk to each other. Sadly they didn't fancy each other, but that's not my fault. Rose left a bit miffed to learn that her story was not going to be commissioned, but she's happy to have met Darren. And Cath and I did all the clearing.

Before everyone arrives

The half an hour when people start arriving is generally the most stressful. Not only are you probably still cooking and/or preparing, you're also trying to be coat-check girl, barman, interested conversationalist and immaculate hostess all at the same time. Not possible. Ask one close friend to arrive a bit earlier to chat and help. Even if they don't do anything beyond laying the table and lighting the candles, it still makes a difference. Otherwise turn the juggling act to your advantage by including people straight away. Men love drinks jobs. I know that's sexist but it's one of the rare times they get to play at being Cary Grant, so it's worth indulging them. Any of them will be at his manliest when asked to open and keep an eye on wine.

Make sure the sink is clear and everything that can be is clean and put away, and the dishwasher, if you have one, is empty. It will help to have as much space as you can for when it comes to clearing the table after you've eaten. Consider putting some kind of container for dirty plates, etc., in the corner of the kitchen out of the way so you can keep the sink clear for filling the kettle, or leaving a hard-to-clean pan to soak. You can pick up old (or new) big enamel bowls in markets and charity shops that would do the trick, hiding the rubble under a tea towel.

Ten minutes before people arrive, drop everything you are doing and go and shut yourself in your bedroom. It doesn't matter if it makes everything ten minutes late. If you can find a bit of time to take a breath, you'll be much calmer and more ordered and efficient when they do arrive. Poise is what you're seeking. If you can pull off Holly Golightly, you'll get the last-minute work done for you.

When everyone arrives

Introduce everyone to each other – you don't need to use surnames if that feels too formal but it's worth dropping in something about either a person they have in common, or work, or an interest. I know I sound like Bridget Jones saying this, but if you give them something to get going with, you'll be able to leave them to it much sooner, and go back to whatever it was you were doing. You probably want to start sitting down about half an hour after they arrive – shorter than that feels like a rush, longer than that involves people keeling over with exhaustion/ starvation/drunkenness. If someone is going to be late, they should call you.

If they don't, give them a call a few minutes before you want to sit down to see what's happened to them – you can just say you're checking to see they're not lost or something and that you'll probably be sitting down to eat soon. If they arrive after you've started, that's their problem.

Serving it up

By the time the food is ready, your priority is to get it to everyone as quickly, neatly and with as little fuss as possible. As far as you can, have everything you need on the table before you sit down. Apart from being aesthetically pleasing, it also means that everyone can help themselves to salad, potatoes and so on. If you don't have room on the table, lay dishes out on a sideboard or surface for everyone to help themselves.

Bear in mind that anything that has been cooked in hot water or is sloppy will give you an impromptu steam facial when you decant it. It's worth asking a man or someone who doesn't wear make-up to do that job. If you don't want to decant food unnecessarily into new bowls for the table, fatly roll a clean tea towel lengthways, wrap it around the outside of the pan and tie the ends together – it will go a long way to making it feel more like a serving dish than a cooking pot.

There comes a moment where you just have to give up and dig into the nearest bottle of wine. For me, it's always once everyone has their main course in front of them. Check you've got everything you need on the table (salt, bread, water, salad), that there's more wine within reach, and that pudding is more or less ready to go, and then forget the mess. By pudding, every available surface will be littered. It doesn't matter – everyone should be having enough fun not to worry about it.

Clearing the table

Guests who make a fuss about clearing are one of my pet hates. Not only does it mean you have to have a battle to get them not to just when you've properly relaxed, but you then have to lose and be grateful about it. To me, it means they're not having enough of a good time and are looking for distraction. However, if someone is really insistent, let them get on with it, and stay at the table chatting to others. Most importantly you don't want the evening to feel disrupted, so when you clear, try not to let more than one person get up to help. Conversely, if you have a lot to do and no one is helping, catch the eye of someone you know well.

Try not to do too much clattering and clearing after dinner. Clearing in the least distracting way possible probably means balancing a couple of plates together rather than scraping and stacking them all at once. Old etiquette dictated that there should be no stacking at all at the table, but that was a lot easier to execute with a butler, two footmen and several maids on hand. Make some space perhaps, and empty overflowing ashtrays, but leave neat pudding ends and chocolate or whatever on the table – people will keep picking while they chat; being too tidy will dissipate the warmth, like switching on the lights at a nightclub.

If the evening has been a happy one, people will linger around the table. Unless you're really squashed, or there's a serious seating mismatch, you shouldn't feel you have to move everyone around, or onto the sofa. I tend not to because I love sitting around a table most of all and find that people will always engineer a chance to move around if they want to. However, the sofa can be a good fall-back if you want to break up a bad seating match, give the evening a new lease of life, or allow a natural break for those anxious to relieve babysitters. Feel your way, there's no rule to it.

Getting rid of everyone

Asking friends to leave if they're having a lovely time is hard. Dad tends to yawn and look at his watch a lot, while others will just hide any remaining booze in the hope that guests will get bored without it. Since we are now a brave new touchy-feely nation of good communicators, it is fine to be straightforward about the evening being over. The simplest thing to do is to ask people how they're getting home and whether they need cabs called.

This might sound strange, but I love that quiet time after the front door has slammed. There's a completeness to it; you get to hold off the world for just a little longer. As guests leave, I hear the rhythms of the street re-establish themselves. The outside world begins to filter back in. By eating at my table, a few more people have knitted themselves into my heart.

SUPPER AROUND THE KITCHEN TABLE

Spring-like and full of hope (61)
Baked garlic with herbed white cheese
Prawn, black pudding and spinach paella
Drunken oranges

A substantial summer supper that works in winter, too (67)
Fish stew with saffroned onions
Pear and almond tart

A Middle Eastern carpet picnic (70)
Spatchcocked quail with cumin and chilli
Middle Eastern salads
Moro's yoghurt cake with pistachios

A half-bought, half-made Indian takeaway (73)
Poppadoms
Fresh cherry tomato relish
Keralan fish moilee
Green beans with ginger
Cardamom yoghurt ice with pomegranate in rosewater

A wintry kitchen gathering (78)
Chops with sage and lemon
Christian's lentils
Cheese and salad

A satisfying yet simple after-work gathering (80)
Rack of lamb with tiny roast potatoes and garlicked cannellini
Deconstructed cheesecake

A slow-cooked wintry supper (83)
Coriander babaganoush
Beef stew with chilli, chocolate and giant garlic croutons
Baked Vacherin and salad

From your kitchen stores (86)
Manuela's spinach risotto
Paddy's Greek yoghurt with dark sugar

Three quick ways with spaghetti (89)
With pancetta, chilli, parsley and lemon
With lemon and basil cream
With clams or mussels

A girls' night in (91)
Prawn, sweet potato and aubergine laksa
Double mango with lime

hen I was growing up, Mum and Dad regularly had people over for dinner. It was a real operation. Mum would stay home from the shop (she was a tailor at the time) to fuss around the house, reaching a taut state of near hysteria in the kitchen. Kate and I would beg to stay up, which never worked on a school-night, though we'd do everything we could to stay awake and watch through the banisters as the guests arrived. It was a big hair competition, and Mum, whose thick auburn hair was helped along by big rollers and one of those mushroom heaters you see in hairdressers, always won (in our opinion). A smooth-looking magician who once came to do after-dinner tricks spent an hour sitting on the stairs with us, boggling us with his disappearing cards.

Eventually, we'd creep back to bed and drift off to the smoke and chatter wafting up the stairs. Everyone would oversleep the next morning and we'd be late to school. Now late-to-school has become late-to-work, but the big hair tradition continues. Like mother, like daughter, I am addicted to my heated rollers; where others lunge for their mascara, they are my five-minute fix.

But, unlike my parents' gatherings back then, I can't think of the last time I went to a 'dinner party' – by which I mean fuss, and twiddly food – unless it was to celebrate a very specific occasion, like a birthday. I can't say I'm too sad about it. Like avocado mousse and pineapple and cheese on a stick, they now seem like a relic of previous generations.

Looking back on it, much of the reason I moved back from America was to be able to jostle around the kitchen table with my friends again. I'd missed the fugged-up windows of a steamy kitchen, the noise and the smoke and the lost hours of sleep, but most of all I'd missed the people. Noisy, grumpy, happy, lonely or bored; old friends were the only people who knew when not to take me seriously. I wanted them back around my table.

Where to start with a kitchen supper

Most gatherings happen randomly – the first person you invite will fix the date, and this will govern who else you invite. You'll want a mixture of people, whether chatty, friendly or interesting (these qualities don't always coexist). People you don't know very well will be more work than old friends, so bear in mind how busy that week is for you, as well as when and where you're going to get the shopping done.

Each day of the week has a different character. People can get quite precious about their Mondays, so it's a good evening for one-to-ones with great friends or siblings. Thursdays on the other hand, are perfect for a big jumble of people that might get out of hand. Everyone happily stays too late and you won't mind having a messy kitchen for a day as the weekend is coming. Beware Fridays. They may seem like a good idea, but everyone is so exhausted that they slump after a single glass of wine. Fridays are also vulnerable to options traders.*

Saturday nights have sense of occasion about them – everyone is rested, and the evening will mostly likely be the focus of the weekend. This is a perfect time to pick something gently cooked and deeply tasty. Stews or slowly roasted joints won't be any more demanding to make than something you can whip up at the last minute (in fact they're often easier) but, like a bunch of unruly teenagers, they will need looking in on from time to time so you need to be around. They also have the benefit of needing less last-minute attention.

Suppers often begin as way of introducing people that you think should meet, sometimes with a view to romance, others because of a common cause or interest. If you want a stimulating evening, you need to mix it up by inviting a combination of couples and singles, people who know each other and those who don't. If you want it to be completely relaxed, invite only those who know each other already. Difficulty lies in inviting a gang who know each other whilst tacking on one or two others who don't – either they'll feel left out, or the group will over-compensate by trying to include them in every conversation and it will all end up feeling forced. In truth, there's an alchemy to combining people that you can't entirely control: sometimes it takes off like magic, sometimes it's a bit of a damp squib. It's worth taking chances – while it may go wrong from time to time, it can also result in unpredictably entertaining combinations.

Your home does not need to be immaculate or in any way unrepresentative of how you live, but have it in a welcoming state. I don't mind at all if I've got a pile

---

Options trader (n): person who won't commit to a plan until the last minute in case something more exciting comes along. Most common amongst single males in the twenty-five to thirty-five age group. Options traders are the biggest single threat to the sanity of a host.

of books on the kitchen counter that haven't yet found their way back to the bookshelf, or chairs that don't match and creased cushions. Whether you like it or not, how you live expresses your character, and there's nothing more welcoming than a home.

During the week, you've probably got a maximum of one-and-a-half hours to get yourself, your home and dinner ready. Whatever your priorities, pay attention to the table first, however simply you lay it – it means guests know they are expected. How you spend the rest of your time depends on what you are like. Kate always emerges at the door in swan-like splendour, with groomed hair, polished stories, but not a clue about what to do with the ingredients she's bought. At Daisy's you'll catch wafts of the most amazing cooking smells before you get through the door, which will generally mean she hasn't had time to change. With both, however, the first thing you see will be a properly laid table with flowers and flickering candlelight. You'll immediately be plied with booze and made to feel like the most interesting person either has ever met, the power of which should never be underestimated.

Some things, however, do make a difference. Your place has to be warm and smell good, the lighting should be gentle, and you need clear surfaces for resting drinks on. Think about your entrance or hall: it's the first thing people will see. It is a good place for plants and a mirror, as well as a scented candle – you'll also want somewhere to stash coats and umbrellas nearby. Bathrooms can easily be forgotten, but a couple of tea lights in front of the mirror and a clean towel make a huge difference.

What to wear

What you wear, along with how you lay the table, will set the mood of the evening. Until quite recently, dinner invitations were quite formal, often issued by post and had very clear instructions about dress code. Now, unless it's for a special occasion or fancy dress, it's rare that there is any kind of dress code for supper. If you don't know your guests very well, they will in all likelihood come a little more formally dressed than people you know well. If you'd rather they didn't, use words like 'relaxed', 'informal' and 'supper' to make the point when you're inviting them – 'dinner' always registers more formally. But if it's a special occasion, or you just want to dress up, say so. Formal clothes don't make a formal atmosphere: that's governed by attitude.

Personally I always try to change because I like to shed the day, but I tend to change 'down' not 'up'. I find that a supper during the week feels most relaxed if I am more underdressed than my guests, partly because a little black number looks ridiculous with an apron, and partly because I have a congenital fear of over-dressing. (This is due to a childhood spent in velvet knickerbockers and those patent leather shoes with the little buttons that were impossible to do up without a special hook. Truly. I've got a photograph of myself with my oldest friend Min when we were five. She is wearing a patchwork shirt with huge collars and fringed suede cowboy flares. She is holding a gun. I am sitting in front of her in a smocked dress with Peter Pan collars and the aforementioned shoes. I am holding a dolly. You don't need to be a shrink to work out why I have spent my adult life in jeans.) But if you want to look great without looking like a try-hard, go for a blow-dry instead of getting all dressed up. I'm not joking. You will carry yourself like a queen.

How I met Ed

I'd been single a long time. Sam was fed up with me whining about it. It was time to set me up, and she had in mind a man, Ed, who she'd met at a christening. 'A really lovely guy,' apparently. This sort of description has always made my heart sink. I've never been one for nice guys; fantasy inclines me more to dark and brooding, with glamorous friends, a degree in engineering and a sideline in kite flying.

She invited him to supper whenever she came up to London but he always said no. Eventually she got so fed up she called their mutual friend to find out what was going on. It turned out, with a bit of digging, that he'd felt uncomfortable about being bombarded with invitations by a married mother of two each time she was away from her family. Sara reassured him that he was not being pursued for an affair, and the next time Sam rang, he accepted.

I didn't hold out high hopes, but this was the plan: she would give a dinner at my house. She would do the shopping, she would invite the guests, she would do the cooking; all I had to do was come home and stick around for a few hours. I couldn't really refuse. I invited Daisy along, partly for moral support, and partly because I thought that between us there'd be twice as much chance of someone being interested. So she and I went out for cocktails beforehand and came home to my savoury-scented house, two martinis the better (as some wit – it may have been Dean Martin – once said, like women's breasts, one martini is too few and three, definitely too many).

Ed loped into the room on the nose of eight, a good head taller than everyone else, messy blonde hair and crumpled trousers, both a little too short. He carried himself tall, as though he was born into a world where everyone is six-foot-seven and he can't work out why he's surrounded by midgets. Friendly, enthusiastic, interested – and definitely not my type. He immediately went over to Daisy and started chatting to her. I was relieved, and got on with helping Sam with the meat she was grilling, attempting to hide behind a large wine glass. Next thing I know, a huge shadow fell over me and I look up to find Ed at my side, offering to help. He had thought Daisy was Sam's sister because they look more alike until she corrected him and he obediently came over to chat me up.

When it came to sitting down, he followed close behind me and sat to my right. Sam had surpassed herself. We ate deliciously smoky babaganoush with freshly toasted sourdough, followed by the tenderest strips of marinated steak, with samphire – an unusual but excellent pairing. There was runny cheese to follow, then ice cream and very fudgy brownies. Ed ate a lot, in a pleasing rather than greedy way. He instinctively made sure everyone's glasses were always full. All I remember, from under the haze of alcohol, was that he asked me a lot of interesting questions. I couldn't have told you what they were the next morning, but I definitely found them interesting. I don't think I talked to whoever was sitting on my other side at all.

After a while, it must have been late, everyone else seemed to melt away. Suddenly it was just me and him in the flickering light of the kitchen. So I went and sat on his lap and I kissed him.

SPRING-LIKE AND FULL OF HOPE
Feeds four, but easy for more

Baked garlic with herbed white cheese

This falls somewhere between a nibble and a very relaxed starter. Add a green salad and it's a great lunch, too.

- 4 whole bulbs garlic, preferably new season wet garlic
- 2 sprigs thyme
- 25g butter
- 4 tablespoons olive oil
- salt and black pepper

for the cheese
- 150g creamy goats' cheese
- 100g Greek yoghurt
- 3 tablespoons chopped mixed herbs, such as thyme, parsley and chives

to serve
- sourdough bread

Preheat the oven to 140°C/gas 1. Cut around the head of the garlic and remove the outer skin from the top, exposing the cloves underneath. Place the bulbs in a baking dish just large enough to fit them in, and tuck in the sprigs of thyme. Dot with the butter and pour over the olive oil. Season well, cover and bake for 40 minutes. Then remove the cover and continue baking for a further hour, basting every 15 minutes, until the cloves are soft, golden and sweet.

Meanwhile, remove the rind of the goats' cheese, if it has any, and mash together (or blend) with the yoghurt and herbs. If you are doing it by hand it will remain quite lumpy but it doesn't matter.

To eat, squeeze out the garlic cloves and spread, along with the herb cheese, onto fresh sourdough or other peasanty bread.

Prawn, black pudding and spinach paella

Paella is truly a whole meal from one pan, both from a cooking and eating perspective. Once I'd realized how versatile it was, I bought myself an authentic paella pan – not expensive – and it's given me a huge amount of use and pleasure, but you can use a large, deep frying or sauté pan, too.

The trick to it is to soften the onion, pepper and garlic mixture for a very long time until it goes sludgy and sweet. You can do this in advance, and even in larger batches and keep it in the freezer.

The most common paella contains chicken, prawns and pork, but it will carry all sorts of variations: artichoke and mushroom for vegetarians, baby broad beans and fresh peas to celebrate the early summer, squid and squid ink for black sophistication.

In this recipe you can replace the prawns with thinly sliced pork fillet, which can be treated exactly the same. By the way, cooking chorizo looks like a normal sausage rather than a salami. Increasingly it is appearing in good supermarkets and delis, but if you can't find it, buy about two-thirds of the weight of the cured salami version, chop it up very small, and add it at the same time as the garlic.

I like to serve this with a huge tomato and red onion salad.

- 7 tablespoons olive oil
- 300g uncooked North Atlantic prawns, shells on
- 150g morcilla (or black pudding), sliced into 1cm rounds
- 100g cooking chorizo, cut up into small pieces
- 2 large Spanish onions, finely chopped
- 1 large red bell pepper, deseeded and finely chopped
- 4 garlic cloves, squashed under the blade of a knife
- 250g paella rice
- 1 heaped teaspoon sweet smoked Spanish paprika
- 900ml chicken stock (preferably fresh)
- 500g spinach, washed and drained (you can use defrosted leaf spinach)
- 1 lemon, cut into wedges
- salt

Put a couple of tablespoons of olive oil in a paella pan or large, deep frying pan and place over a high heat. Stir-fry the prawns for a few minutes until nearly, but not quite, cooked. Remove with a slotted spoon and set aside. Fry off any watery

liquid, then add more olive oil and gently fry the black pudding for a couple of minutes, removing it to a separate plate as carefully as you can (it may fall apart but don't worry too much).

In the rest of the oil, fry the chorizo for a couple of minutes, then add the onion and bell pepper. You need to fry these, stirring frequently, until they reduce and caramelize (see note above) – at first on a fairly high heat but after 5 minutes, turn it right down to cook very slowly. It will take longer than you expect and for a while they will seem to steam more than fry, but have faith – they will reduce and sweeten in about 35–40 minutes.

After half an hour, when they look nearly done, add the garlic and continue cooking for another 5–10 minutes until the mixture is really soft and sweet. Add the rice, stir well to coat and sprinkle evenly with the paprika. Season with salt but keep in mind that if you're using chicken stock from a cube or granules it will be much saltier than fresh. Until this point you can make the dish in advance.

About 25 minutes before you are ready to eat, heat the chicken stock until nearly boiling and let the rice mixture warm through. Lay the black pudding over the top of the rice and pour the hot stock gently into the paella pan. Bring to a gentle bubble and leave it – the rice should not be disturbed from this point on, or it will break down and go mushy.

In the meantime, in a large saucepan, wilt the spinach (if you are using fresh), with just the water drops left on it from washing and a heavy-handed pinch of salt. Squeeze out any water and set aside with the prawns. If using defrosted spinach, skip this step.

Taste the rice after 20 minutes – you want it to be almost cooked but with very little bite left. When it seems just done there should be only a little liquid around the edge of the pan. Switch off the burner. Scatter the prawns and then the spinach over the rice and push down with your fingers – be careful, it'll be really hot. Cover firmly with a large piece of tin foil and leave to rest for 5 minutes before serving with a segment of lemon.

Drunken oranges

This is the pudding I fall back on mid-week as you can even make it at the table if you haven't got around to doing it in advance. I particularly love using blood oranges when they're in season as they look so beautiful, but any good eating oranges work as well. It's like the seventies favourite oranges in caramel, but fresher tasting. I like to serve this with 'homemade' brownies from the deli, chopped up into bite-sized squares and piled onto a plate in the middle of the table, or even a bar of chocolate.

- 4 oranges
- 150ml pudding wine (or 75ml triple sec or Grand Marnier)
- small handful mint leaves, shredded

- sugar, to taste

to serve
- cream or ice cream

Cut the top and bottom off the oranges so that a little flesh is exposed. To peel, stand on one end and cut downwards just underneath the pith to shave it off. Once completely rid of pith and skin, slice the oranges across into slender rounds. Put them in a glass bowl if you have one, including any juice you can save, and pour over a good glug of your chosen booze, so that they're more or less immersed.

Scatter over the mint leaves, and sugar if you think you need it, and leave to steep for as long as you've got. Serve with cream or ice cream, which will curdle a little and in doing so will look strangely beautiful on the plate.

A SUBSTANTIAL SUMMER SUPPER
THAT WORKS IN WINTER, TOO
Feeds eight

Fish stew with saffroned onions

I like to use a mixture of conger eel, red mullet and gurnard fillets with mussels here, as they are tasty, cheap and not under threat from over-fishing. The stew has a really deep flavour – if you're not afraid of raw garlic, add more to the parsley pistou. You can either stir it in at the end of cooking or leave it in a separate bowl for everyone to help themselves. Accompany this dish with good bread, butter (or olive oil, but I like butter here to temper the Mediterranean flavours a bit), and a clean fennel-based salad, if you like.

- 8 tablespoons olive oil
- 2 red bell peppers, deseeded and thinly sliced
- 4 large Spanish onions, thinly sliced
- 2 tablespoons thyme leaves
- 2 tablespoons rosemary leaves, very finely chopped
- 3 bay leaves
- 2 large pinches saffron strands
- 1 teaspoon sweet smoked Spanish paprika
- 20 new potatoes
- 250ml white wine or Fino sherry
- 1 x 400g tin plum tomatoes, drained and chopped (or 4 fresh ones, skinned and deseeded)

- 600ml fish stock (see page 266)
- 100g ground almonds, lightly toasted (optional)
- 1kg firm white fish in large pieces
- 1kg mussels or clams
- salt and black pepper

for the pistou
- 2 garlic cloves
- 60g flat-leafed parsley, leaves picked and finely chopped
- 5 tablespoons olive oil

Warm the olive oil in a casserole. Add the bell pepper, onions, thyme, rosemary, bay, saffron and paprika and cook gently, without letting them colour, until the vegetables are very soft, stirring regularly to prevent sticking and burning. Warning: this will take 30–40 minutes.

In a separate saucepan, boil the new potatoes in salted water until nearly cooked, about 10 minutes depending on their size.

Turn the heat up on the onions, add the wine and let the alcohol bubble off, then reduce the heat again and add the tomatoes and fish stock. Simmer for 5 minutes. Turn off the heat, stirring in the almonds if you'd like a thicker sauce, and season well. You can do all of the above up to a day in advance, then cover and store in the fridge until you're ready.

Fifteen minutes before you're ready to eat, bring the sauce back to a gentle simmer. Meanwhile, using a pestle and mortar, pound the garlic and parsley together with some salt and the olive oil until you have a paste.

Add the fish and shellfish to the sauce, making sure the white fish is covered in sauce – the shellfish can sit on the top to steam if needs be. Cover and simmer for 5 minutes, then add the potatoes and cook for a further 5 minutes. Stir in the garlic and parsley paste, then taste and season if necessary. Switch off the heat and leave the stew to stand for a further 5 minutes before serving.

Pear and almond tart

This is Daisy's adaptation of the River Café tart. Her tip is to use pears as ripe as you can find and to pack in as many as you can: it makes a big difference to the lightness and freshness of the tart.

for the pastry
- 175g plain flour, plus extra for dusting
- 50g icing sugar
- pinch salt
- 100g chilled unsalted butter, cubed, plus extra for greasing
- 2 egg yolks

for the filling
- 175g blanched almonds
- 175g unsalted butter, soft
- 175g caster sugar
- 2 eggs
- 7 ripe pears, peeled, halved and cored

First make the pastry by sifting together the flour, icing sugar and salt, and pulsing them together with the butter in a food processor. As soon as the mixture resembles fine breadcrumbs, add the egg yolks, and run the machine briefly until the pastry comes together in a ball – you may need a tablespoon of cold water, too. Wrap in clingfilm and leave to rest for at least an hour – or overnight – in the fridge.

When you are ready to bake the tart, preheat the oven to 180°C/gas 4 and grease a 28cm loose-bottomed tart tin. On a cool, floured surface, roll out the pastry as thin as you can – about 2–3mm thick.

Using the rolling pin to help you, lift the pastry and drape it over the tart tin, easing it into the corners and up the sides. Cut off any excess pastry around the rim. Prick the base all over with a fork. Line the tart case with parchment paper and baking beans and bake blind for 10 minutes. Then remove the parchment and beans and bake for a further 10 minutes, until the case turns light golden. Remove the tart case from the oven and turn down the temperature to 150°C/gas 2.

Meanwhile, make the filling. Grind the almonds in the processor till fine, and set aside. Either by hand, in a processor, or with a food mixer, cream the butter and sugar together until pale and light. Add the almonds, mixing well, then add the eggs one by one. If you are using a processor, you will need to scrape down the sides with a spatula from time to time to make sure everything is well combined.

Lay the pears face down over the pastry case – you will probably fit 6 of them in. In this case, chop up the last one into smaller bits and pack it into the spaces. Pour over the almond mixture and smooth the surface. Bake for 1 hour, checking after 50 minutes – when it's ready the surface should be golden brown. If it's still not done after an hour, finish with a quick blast under the grill. Cool before serving.

A MIDDLE EASTERN CARPET PICNIC
Feeds six

Spatchcocked quail with cumin and chilli

Free-range quail are significantly larger (more juicy and delicious, too) than battery ones, so you'll need to adjust the cooking time and the number you need accordingly. You can cook them on a griddle pan, barbecue, or under an overhead grill, but if you are using direct heat, be careful not set it too high as the flesh is delicate. Serve the quail accompanied by the Persian rice on page 198, or the flatbread on page 271.

- 3 tablespoons cumin seeds
- 4 dried chillies, crumbled
- 3 tablespoons sea salt
- 12–15 quail
- olive oil

Toast the cumin seeds in a dry frying pan over a medium-high heat for a few minutes, shaking to turn frequently. When they begin to release their scent, remove to a mortar and pound until you have a grainy powder. Crumble in the dried chillies and sea salt and mix through.

To spatchcock the quail, cut down the backbone (you can do this with any pair of kitchen scissors, the bones are easy to cut through) and splay the birds out flat. The breasts will now be next to each other and the legs and wings at each side. Remove any remaining guts or little sacs dangling underneath, wash all over and pat dry, being careful not to split the fragile skin.

Preheat a griddle pan, barbecue or overhead grill. Brush the quail with the very meanest amount of olive oil. Rub the spice mix evenly over the birds on both sides. Cook the breast side first for 5–7 minutes (depending on the size of the birds), then turn over and do the same on the underside – the flesh should be juicy but not pink.

Leave to rest for a few minutes before serving so they can be eaten in your fingers – either hot, warm or cold.

Middle Eastern salads

I like this to be a half-bought, half-made sort of supper, supplementing the quails with these and other Middle Eastern dips and salads depending on how many people I have coming.

- Tabbouleh
- Tzatziki
- Houmous

If you have time and enjoy chopping, you could make the tabbouleh and tzatziki from scratch from the recipes on page 182 and page 183. Otherwise, buy them all and perk them up with a squeeze of lemon juice, a few drops of olive oil and some freshly chopped coriander, mint or parsley.

Moro's yoghurt cake with pistachios

This is from the first Moro book. At times it comes out firmer than at others, but the correct consistency is a light sponge with wet custard underneath. It should be eaten at room temperature so can be made a few hours in advance. This recipe will fit a 25cm round or square baking tin.

- 3 large eggs, separated
- 70g caster sugar
- 1 vanilla pod, split in half lengthways
- 350g Greek yoghurt
- finely grated zest and juice of 1 unwaxed lemon
- finely grated zest of 1/2 unwaxed orange

- 1 heaped teaspoon plain flour
- 30g shelled unsalted pistachio nuts, roughly chopped

to serve

- 1 tablespoon edible rose petals (optional)
- 120g Greek yoghurt

Preheat the oven to 180°C/gas 4 and put a bain-marie of water in to warm (I just use a part-filled roasting tin). Line your baking tin with greaseproof paper.

Put the egg yolks, 50g of the sugar and the seeds of the vanilla pod into a bowl and beat until thick and pale. Add the yoghurt, lemon zest and juice, orange zest, and flour and mix well. Set aside.

In a large, clean bowl whisk the egg whites until soft peaks have formed, then whisk in the remaining sugar. Fold the whites into the yoghurt mixture with a metal spoon, then spoon the mixture into your baking tin.

Place the tin in the bain-marie, making sure the hot water comes halfway up the sides of the tin, and bake for about 10 minutes. Sprinkle the pistachios on top and return to the oven to cook for a further 10–15 minutes or until the top is golden and just firm.

Scatter with torn rose petals and serve with yoghurt.

A HALF-BOUGHT, HALF-MADE INDIAN TAKEAWAY
Feeds eight to ten

The bought bit
Ask a guest to pick up these extras from an Indian restaurant on their way over:

- Mango chutney
- Raita
- Naan or chapattis
- Rice

Poppadoms
The idea of this supper is to make only as much as you have time for, so you could buy poppadoms from your local Indian restaurant, along with chapattis and rice. However, I find them easy and fun to make and I enjoy the last-minute flashiness. Southern Indians always use coconut oil to cook poppadoms, which gives them a distinctive fragrance, but you may prefer unscented vegetable or groundnut oil. Serve with mango chutney, and the fresh cherry tomato relish below, if you have time to make it.

- 1 packet uncooked poppadoms
- coconut oil, or vegetable oil

Heat 2.5cm of oil in a large, deep frying pan until very hot. Drop a poppadom in – it will pop and spit and double in size before your very eyes, like a Shrink-y-dink in reverse. As soon as it seems fully blown (this takes a matter of seconds) fish it out with a pair of tongs and allow the oil to drip off before setting the poppadom on a plate and getting to work on the next. You may need to turn it over and briefly cook the other side if the oil hasn't reached every part.

Serve when you've got a stack of 4 or 5 to get everyone going – you can continue as necessary, but keep an eye on the hot oil.

Fresh cherry tomato relish

This can work equally well as a salsa with the poppadoms, or just as a salad to serve on the side of the curry.

- 500g cherry tomatoes
- 40g coriander, chopped
- 1 red chilli, finely chopped
- 1/2 red onion, finely chopped

- 2 tablespoons olive oil
- juice of 1/2 lime
- salt and black pepper

Cut the tomatoes in half and put them in a mixing bowl. Add the other ingredients and toss well.

Keralan fish moilee

A lovely Indian cook taught this simple Southern Indian curry to me when I went travelling there. You'll want some rice to serve it with, and if you have a local curry house, get a guest to pick up some chapattis on their way to you.

- 6 tablespoons coconut oil (or groundnut oil)
- 1 teaspoon cumin seeds
- 1 teaspoon black mustard seeds
- 6 small red onions, thinly sliced
- 4 large garlic cloves, finely chopped
- 6 green chillies, thinly sliced
- 15cm fresh ginger, peeled and finely chopped

- 1 teaspoon turmeric powder
- 1.6 litres coconut milk
- 8 curry leaves (fresh if you can find them)
- 1.75kg meaty fish such as monkfish or conger eel, cut into 3–4cm chunks
- 20 cherry tomatoes
- sea salt and black pepper

Heat the oil in a large, heavy-based saucepan, and fry the cumin and mustard seeds for a couple of minutes until they crackle and pop. Add the onion, garlic, chillies and ginger and cook until they are soft but not caramelized, about 15 minutes. You may need to turn the heat down a little after 5 minutes to prevent burning.

Add the turmeric, coconut milk and curry leaves, and season to taste – you'll need a fair amount of salt to counter the sweetness of the coconut milk and bring out the flavours of all the herbs and spices. Bring to the boil, then turn the heat down so that it's barely simmering – or turn it off if you are preparing in advance.

About 15 minutes before you are ready to eat, reheat the sauce if necessary, and when it is hot, add the fish. Bring back to a gentle simmer and poach the fish for about 10 minutes. Just before serving, add the tomatoes.

Green beans with ginger

If you're not in the mood for much chopping, you can keep the beans whole. They can be cooked in advance and gently reheated, or served immediately. This recipe is based on one from *The Essential Madhur Jaffrey*.

- 675g fresh green beans
- 5cm fresh ginger, peeled and roughly chopped
- 6 tablespoons vegetable oil
- $^1/_4$ teaspoon turmeric powder
- $^1/_2$ fresh green chilli, very finely sliced
- 2 teaspoons ground coriander
- 1 teaspoon ground cumin
- 3 tablespoons chopped fresh coriander leaves
- 1 teaspoon garam masala
- 2 teaspoons lemon juice (or to taste)
- salt

Top and tail the beans, chop into 3–5mm rounds and set aside in a bowl. Blend or pound the ginger with 3 tablespoons of water to give a smooth paste.

Heat the oil in a frying pan and add the ginger paste and turmeric. Fry, stirring constantly, for 2 minutes, then add the chilli and ground coriander, and after another minute, the beans. Continue cooking and stirring for about a minute, then add the cumin, coriander leaves, garam masala, lemon juice, salt and 3 tablespoons of warm water.

Cover the pan, turn the heat right down and let the beans cook slowly for about 40 minutes, stirring every so often.

Cardamom yoghurt ice with pomegranate in rosewater

This recipe could be served as a scented yoghurt instead of freezing it, which makes it both exotic and extremely simple. Frozen, it is not as rich as egg-based ice cream, and has a delightful tang. Serve with pomegranate seeds tossed with a little sugar and rosewater, or if you can't find pomegranates, some tinned lychees drained of most of the syrup would work well, too. (I find them the only bearable tinned fruit.)

- 12 green cardamom pods
- 1 litre Greek yoghurt
- 4–5 tablespoons condensed milk

to serve
- seeds of 2 pomegranates
- 2 tablespoons rosewater
- 1 tablespoon caster sugar

Crush the cardamom pods with a pestle and mortar and pick out the green husks before pounding the black seeds to a fine powder. Combine the yoghurt and condensed milk in a mixing bowl, stir in the cardamom and taste to check for sweetness – I like it quite tart, but you may prefer to add extra condensed milk.

Churn the mixture in an ice cream machine, if you have one. Alternatively pour it into a plastic container and freeze, stirring every half an hour to prevent large ice crystals forming. This will take a couple of hours and you will need to let it soften a little outside the freezer before eating.

Just before serving, toss the pomegranate seeds with the rosewater and caster sugar in a bowl and take to the table for everyone to sprinkle over their ice cream.

A WINTRY KITCHEN GATHERING
Feeds four

Chops with sage and lemon

The longer you have to marinate the meat, the better the flavour will be. An hour is OK, overnight is great, but allow it to come back to room temperature before you cook. Serve with the lentils below and dark greens.

- 4 veal or pork chops, cut thick (2.5–3cm)
- juice and pared zest of 1 unwaxed lemon
- 1 tablespoon fresh chopped sage, or 2 tablespoons dried sage

- 4 tablespoons olive oil
- salt and black pepper

to serve
- paprika, for sprinkling
- chopped parsley, for sprinkling

Place the chops in a large Ziploc plastic bag. Whisk the lemon juice, zest, sage, oil and seasoning together and pour into the bag. Leave to marinate in the fridge for as long as you have.

Under a medium-hot grill, cook the chops for 10 minutes on each side. Check for readiness (pork should be succulent but not pink, veal can be rarer) and grill for a further 5 minutes if necessary.

Leave the chops to stand for 5 minutes before serving with a little paprika and chopped parsley sprinkled over them.

Christian's lentils

My friend Christian looks like a French boy (drainpipe jeans, dirty gymshoes) and cooks like one too. I love these lentils, which can be a meal in themselves with a little goats' cheese crumbled on top, or work beautifully with fish, or pork chops. Make in a big batch as they will keep well in the fridge for a week.

- 1 bulb garlic, cloves separated but not peeled
- 1 celery stick, not too finely chopped
- 1 carrot, not too finely chopped
- olive oil
- 100g pancetta (or bacon), cubed
- 300g Puy lentils
- 500ml chicken stock (preferably fresh)
- 1/2 glass beer (preferably ordinary lager)
- sea salt and black pepper

Place a saucepan over a moderate heat. When hot, throw in the garlic, celery and carrot with a big glug of olive oil. After a few minutes, add the pancetta and cook until it begins to brown. Add the lentils and stir vigorously until they are well covered in the oil and flavourings. Season with generous amounts of salt and pepper and cook, stirring, for about 5 minutes.

Pour in the stock, stir, then add enough water so that there is twice the level of liquid to lentils in the pan. Bring to the boil then lower the heat so that the lentils simmer until almost all the liquid has evaporated. The dish is done when the lentils are melting into a thick mass but still have a little individual bite – it will take about 30–40 minutes (the packet will say less, but I find them indigestible when too al dente). You can add water as necessary during cooking, or drain them, within reason.

At the last moment, add a good glug or two of beer – this is done to your own taste, but it's important that the beer should add a little bite to the flavours without overpowering them. Take the pan off the heat and allow to cool for a short while before serving.

Cheese and salad

The French always save their salad to eat with cheese, and it makes a wonderful accompaniment. Buy one runny cheese and one firm, and serve on a plate with some crackers, accompanied by a green salad.

A SATISFYING YET SIMPLE
AFTER-WORK GATHERING
Feeds six

Rack of lamb with tiny roast potatoes and garlicked cannellini

If I had to name one, rack of lamb would be my favoured cut. It's not the cheapest but I can extol its many-purposed brilliance to solve almost any situation and there are few who don't love it. Marinate this for as long as you can – overnight preferably – but it's still worth making even if you only have time to slather on the marinade and bang it immediately in the oven. Serve with a salad or something green, plus the classic redcurrant jelly and mint sauce if you like.

for the lamb
- 6 garlic cloves, crushed to a paste with salt
- 4 sprigs rosemary, finely chopped
- 1 tin anchovies
- 4 tablespoons olive oil
- 3 racks of lamb (about 18 cutlets) – ask for French trim but leave off the white hats
- salt and black pepper

for the potatoes
- 6 large or 12 medium potatoes, cut into 1cm cubes
- 4–6 garlic cloves, unpeeled
- 2 or 3 sprigs rosemary
- 2 tablespoons olive oil

for the beans
- 2 x 400g tins cannellini beans, drained with a few tablespoons of liquid reserved

Mash together the garlic, rosemary, anchovies and olive oil, and season with salt and pepper.

Rub three-quarters of the mixture generously in and around the lamb racks, getting into any crevices between the meat and bone that you can find or would like to make. Leave to marinate for as long as you can.

Preheat the oven to 220°C/gas 7. In a large roasting pan, toss the potato cubes, garlic cloves and rosemary sprigs thoroughly in olive oil and sprinkle with salt.

Make space in the middle to stand the lamb, bones pointing up. About 45 minutes before you want to eat, roast for 22–26 minutes depending on how well done you like the lamb (22 will be a deep rose, 26 the medium side of rare. I like mine on the nose of 24).

Take out the lamb and wrap it with foil, making a baggy but firmly sealed packet, and leave to stand somewhere warm (such as on top of the oven or hob) for 20 minutes. Give the potatoes a good shake and return them to the oven for a further 20 minutes, checking and turning once more during cooking.

Meanwhile, in a saucepan, gently fry the remaining garlic-rosemary-anchovy mixture for a couple of minutes until it softens and tempers. Add the drained beans and reserved liquid and warm through, stirring and mashing so that some of the beans break up. Add a little extra olive oil if you'd like to. Turn off the heat (the beans can be served warm or at room temperature).

After 20 minutes, the potatoes should be golden all over. Divide them between serving plates, or empty into a bowl for people to help themselves. Unwrap the lamb and carve into individual cutlets, which should be a perfect pink inside. Serve with the cannellini beans, redcurrant jelly and mint sauce, and a soft green salad or vegetable.

Deconstructed cheesecake

This is not a traditional cheesecake as it doesn't set: it's more the familiar biscuity base with a slightly sweetened creamy topping. Finished off with some kind of fruit, it is pretty much the easiest pudding imaginable. You can replace the digestives with whichever biscuits take your fancy: gingernuts, hobnobs or orange or lemon butter biscuits all work well. Use a loose-bottomed cake tin that is about 22cm in diameter.

- 250g digestives
- 120g butter
- 300g mascarpone
- 300g Greek yoghurt
- 50g caster sugar

to serve
- 2 punnets fresh berries, fruit compote, or a jar of good bottled fruit in syrup

Preheat the oven to 180°C/gas 4. Crush the biscuits to a fine powder either, as tradition dictates, in a plastic bag with a rolling pin, or in a whizzer.

Melt the butter in a saucepan and add the biscuits to it, stirring until well blended. Smooth evenly into a loose-bottomed cake tin so that the biscuit base is about 1cm thick, or a little more. Bake for ten minutes, then transfer to the fridge or freezer to cool and set.

Meanwhile, to make the topping, beat together the mascarpone, yoghurt and sugar in a large mixing bowl.

Remove the base from the cake tin, lay it on a serving plate and spoon over the topping, not caring in the least that it lazily pools over the sides. Top with whatever fruit you have chosen, then divide and serve.

For a slightly more elegant version, serve the mascarpone-yoghurt mixture and the fruit in bowls, with the biscuit base cut up on the side.

A SLOW-COOKED WINTRY SUPPER
Feeds eight

Coriander babaganoush

Babaganoush is a silky, smoky Middle Eastern aubergine dip. The trick is to really char the aubergine, which will infuse it with the all-important smoky flavour.

Warning: the aubergines do take quite a while to grill properly, so if you're planning this for an after-work mid-week dinner, either make it the day before (adding the coriander at the last minute), or substitute this dish with bought houmous, which you can perk up with extra lemon juice, olive oil, a spoonful of tahini, a handful of fresh coriander, and a sprinkling of cayenne or paprika.

- 3 large aubergines, or 4 medium ones
- 1–2 garlic cloves, crushed to a paste with 1 teaspoon salt
- juice of 1 lemon
- 5 tablespoons tahini
- 2 heaped tablespoons chopped fresh coriander leaves

- 4 tablespoons olive oil
- sea salt

to serve
- toasted pitta or homemade flatbread (see page 271)

Pierce the skins of the aubergines to prevent them exploding, and grill whole. This is easiest over a hot barbecue if you have a gas one, otherwise put them on a griddle pan, or under the grill, turning every so often, until the skin is charred and crisp all over and the flesh is collapsing. Even better, if you have time, is to spear them with a toasting fork and cook in the flame of your gas hob or fire.

Remove the aubergines from the heat and set aside until cool enough to handle. Cut off the tops, then peel and discard the papery layer of charred skin. Put the flesh and any juices in a mixing bowl. Add the rest of the ingredients and beat with a whisk or fork until nearly smooth.

Serve the dip with torn pieces of lightly toasted pitta, or homemade flatbread.

Beef stew with chilli, chocolate and giant garlic croutons

There are no two ways about it: this recipe is for cooking in advance. The joy is that you then need do nothing but reheat it in the oven and make the garlic croutons. Made with steak-sized pieces of meat rather than small cubes, it's surprisingly elegant as long as you don't drip gravy everywhere when you dish it up. Serve with plain boiled cabbage to offset the richness; you might want some mash, too, if you've got a very hungry bunch to feed.

- olive oil or dripping
- 1.75kg chuck roast or braising steak, cut into thick portions (think of small steaks, not stewing cubes)
- 2 carrots, chopped
- 2 celery sticks, chopped
- 4 large onions, chopped
- 6 garlic cloves, squashed under the blade of a knife
- 800ml fresh beef stock and/or red wine (in whichever combination you prefer)

- 3 dried bird's-eye chillies, crumbled
- small bunch thyme
- 1½ tablespoons Dijon mustard
- 30–40g very good, dark chocolate, at least 70 per cent cocoa solids
- sea salt and black pepper

for the croutons
- 2 whole bulbs garlic
- 125g butter, soft
- 2 baguettes, cut very diagonally into large pieces 4cm thick

Heat the oven to 150°C/gas 2. In batches in a large casserole, heat the olive oil or dripping and brown the meat carefully, seasoning well as you go, removing the pieces to a plate when done. Add a little more oil or dripping to the casserole and soften the carrots, celery and onions over a medium heat for about 10 minutes. Add the garlic and continue frying for a further 5 minutes or until it turns golden.

Return the meat to the pan, along with the red wine and/or stock, chillies, thyme, Dijon mustard and plenty of black pepper. Bring to a simmer then cover and transfer the casserole to the oven for 2 hours. Cut the top off the garlic bulbs, put them in a small roasting dish and place in the oven for 1½ hours.

Remove the garlic and set aside until cool enough to handle. Squeeze the now-softened garlic cloves from their skins and mash with the butter. Spread the mixture over one side of each slice of baguette.

When the stew is nearly ready, stir in the chocolate, making sure it melts evenly into the sauce – it should add richness but shouldn't overwhelm it. Sit as many of the garlic-buttered bread slices on top of the stew as you can fit in one layer, so they can soak up the juices. Put any you can't fit in the pot on a baking sheet. Leave the lid off the casserole and place it, and the sheet of croutons, in the oven for a final 5–10 minutes. Remove when the bread is golden and just toasted on top. Serve the extra croutons alongside the stew, with plenty of sauce and some cabbage.

Baked Vacherin and salad

I remember the first time I tasted Vacherin. It was at a dinner, and there was a huge one in the middle of the table for everyone to share. The whole cheese ended up on my plate with me eating it directly from its wooden tub with a spoon. It took me a while to realize that everyone was staring at me, and I still blush at the memory.

You'll only be able to find Vacherin from November through until March. If it is properly ripe, you'll be able to scoop it out with a spoon, cold or warm, but it's fun to bake it, and this ensures that it will run even if it's not totally ripe. The cheese comes in two sizes – the smaller will serve about four people after dinner (or two or three people for supper or lunch), the larger will feed twelve. If you buy a slice rather than a whole cheese, wrap it firmly in foil before baking.

- 1 whole Vacherin cheese
- 1 clove garlic, unpeeled and squashed under the blade of a knife (optional)
- 1 sprig rosemary

to serve
- salad and/or bread

Preheat the oven to 180°C/gas 4. Make a hole in the middle of the cheese and push in the garlic and rosemary (if you have an open bottle of white wine, add a few drops of that, too). Cover loosely with foil, and bake for 15 minutes, or 20 if it's a big cheese.

Remove from the oven and serve the cheese hot, spooned over salad or bread.

FROM YOUR KITCHEN STORES
Feeds four

Manuela's spinach risotto

This is the risotto we ate growing up, when we wouldn't eat greens. It is not an authentic risotto but it is wonderfully tasty and very easy. You can even make it with normal long-grain rice if you don't have risotto rice handy, as the consistency is appealingly soupy. If you don't have any cream, stir in a knob of butter at the end.

- 450g risotto rice
- 750g frozen spinach
- $^1/_2$ teaspoon freshly grated nutmeg
- 1 chicken stock cube
- 50ml double cream
- 150g Parmesan cheese, grated
- salt and black pepper

Boil a full kettle of water. Put the rice in a large saucepan, cover with the boiled water and bring to a simmer. Cook at a bare burble for about 25–30 minutes, stirring frequently and adding a little hot water from time to time, just enough to keep it covered.

Meanwhile, put the frozen spinach in a large pan with a little water and cook until it has just defrosted. Remove from the heat and stir in the nutmeg. Whiz the spinach with a blender until smooth, then set aside.

When the rice is soft and creamy, crumble in the stock cube and a few good grinds of pepper and stir to disperse. Add the spinach, mix well and taste for seasoning. It will probably want at least a teaspoon of salt.

When you are ready to eat, stir in the cream and half the Parmesan, and serve the rest of the Parmesan in a bowl for people to help themselves.

Paddy's Greek yoghurt with dark sugar

You can replace the mango and passionfruit with any soft fruit or berries.

- 1 large ripe mango
- 500ml Greek yoghurt

- 2 passionfruit, halved
- 4 tablespoons dark muscovado sugar

Peel and chop the mango into 1cm cubes and split between four cups or tumblers. Put a generous spoonful of yoghurt on top of each, then a thin layer of sugar, and smooth out to the edges. Empty the seeds of each half-passionfruit into each cup, then top up with yoghurt. Sprinkle the rest of the dark sticky sugar over the top of each one – you may need to crumble it with your fingers as it tends to clag together.

Cover and put in the fridge for as long as you can so that the sugar sinks and streaks throughout – a couple of hours is preferable. Eat straight from the cup.

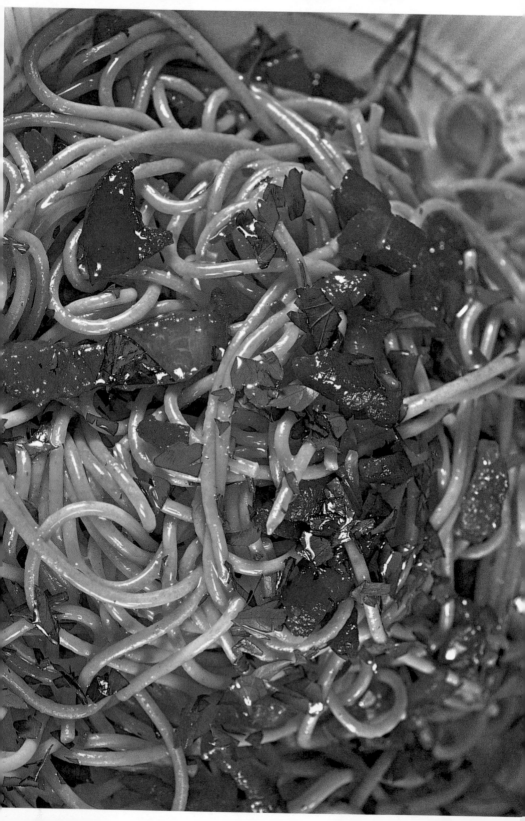

THREE QUICK WAYS WITH SPAGHETTI
Feeds four each

With pancetta, chilli, parsley and lemon

This is one of the easiest pasta dishes to throw together at no notice – the sauce barely needs cooking – making it perfect for any unexpected drop-in. There's something inspiring about the heat of the chillies, the slipperiness of the olive oil and the grassiness of the parsley.

- 400g spaghetti
- 250g pancetta
- olive oil
- 3 garlic cloves, very finely chopped
- 3 red chillies, very finely chopped

- pared zest of 1 unwaxed lemon, cut into fine strips
- large handful flat-leafed parsley, chopped
- 150g Parmesan cheese, grated
- sea salt and black pepper

Bring a large pan of water to the boil. Just before you add the spaghetti, throw in a generous amount of salt – the water should be as salty as the Mediterranean. Cook according to the packet instructions, but begin to taste for readiness a minute before it's due to be cooked. You want it al dente, but not raw in the middle.

Meanwhile, fry the pancetta in a lug of olive oil over a reasonably high heat for a few minutes, stirring until it starts to colour. Turn the heat down and add the garlic, chillies and lemon zest, stirring and frying for a couple of minutes.

When the spaghetti is done, drain it, reserving a tablespoon of the cooking water in the pan with the pasta, and toss together with the oily, garlicky pancetta mixture and the parsley. Serve with plenty of Parmesan and some freshly ground black pepper, too.

With lemon and basil cream

This is pretty much a kitchen cupboard supper in the summer, when fragrant basil is abundant. Great for vegetarians, and needs nothing but a green salad to accompany and some fruit to follow.

- 400g spaghetti
- pared zest of 2 unwaxed lemons, cut into fine strips
- 2 egg yolks
- 4 tablespoons olive oil
- 150ml double cream
- 50g basil leaves, roughly torn
- 100g Parmesan cheese, finely grated
- sea salt and black pepper

Cook the spaghetti as on page 89. Meanwhile, stir together the rest of the ingredients, seasoning generously. When the spaghetti is cooked, drain it, reserving a tablespoon of the cooking water in the pan, and toss thoroughly with the sauce.

With clams or mussels

Without the spaghetti, this becomes a classic treatment for shellfish, which you could split between two, mopping up the fragrant juices with crusty bread.

- 400g spaghetti
- 3 tablespoons olive oil
- 25g butter
- 3 garlic cloves, finely chopped
- 1 small red chilli, very finely sliced
- 1.5kg clams or mussels, or a mixture
- 150ml white wine
- handful flat-leafed parsley, chopped
- sea salt and black pepper

Cook the spaghetti as on page 89. Meanwhile, in a large, lidded saucepan, warm the olive oil and butter and fry the garlic and chilli together for a couple of minutes. Add the shellfish and wine, cover and allow to steam for about 3 minutes, shaking from time to time to prevent sticking.

Drain the spaghetti when it is cooked and toss with the shellfish, sprinkling over the parsley and seasoning to taste. I like Parmesan with it, though purists will shudder.

A GIRLS' NIGHT IN
Feeds four

Prawn, sweet potato and aubergine laksa

The spice paste used here is easiest made in a whizzer. It will stick up the sides, so you'll need to keep stopping to push it down with a spatula, and it may need a teaspoon of water to help it along. Alternatively, you could chop the ingredients finely, or pound them with a pestle and mortar; it will take some effort but you may find it therapeutic. These days it is quite easy to buy ready-cooked rice noodles in vacuum-packs, but if you can't find them, use other rice noodles and cook them according to the packet instructions. For vegetarians, omit the prawns and replace the chicken stock with vegetable stock.

- 500ml chicken or vegetable stock
- 400ml coconut milk
- 200g large uncooked North Atlantic prawns, shells and heads on
- 2 sweet potatoes, peeled and cut into 1–2cm chunks
- 1 large aubergine, cut into 1–2cm chunks
- 100g fresh cooked rice noodles, or 50g dried
- 3 red chillies, deseeded and finely chopped
- 2 garlic cloves, finely chopped
- 5cm fresh ginger, peeled and chopped
- 1 stalk lemongrass, woody end removed, and chopped
- 20–40g fresh coriander, roughly chopped
- 2 tablespoons coconut or vegetable oil
- 20 cherry tomatoes
- 2 tablespoons Thai fish sauce
- juice of $^1/_2$ lime
- salt and black pepper

Warm the stock and coconut milk together in a saucepan. Detach the heads of the prawns from the bodies and add the heads to the liquid along with the sweet potato and aubergine. Simmer very gently for 20 minutes while you set about doing the rest.

If necessary, cook the noodles according to the packet instructions. Drain, then run them under cold water and set aside. Meanwhile, pound, whiz or very finely chop together the chillies, garlic, ginger, lemongrass and half the coriander so that you have a paste.

In a large saucepan, heat the oil and fry 2 tablespoons of the spice paste for 3–4 minutes, stirring so it doesn't stick.

Remove the prawn heads from the coconut milk mixture then add it and the vegetables to the spice paste. You can do everything up until this point in advance, covering all the ingredients and setting them aside to cool until you're ready to eat.

A few minutes before you eat, warm the liquid and vegetables till just murmuring. Drop in the cherry tomatoes and prawns and simmer gently for a couple of minutes.

Add the cooked noodles, fish sauce and lime juice to the laksa and divide between serving bowls, sprinkling over the rest of the coriander. Adjust the seasonings to taste and serve.

Double mango with lime

There's no cooking to this pudding: it's a simple exercise in assembly. The squeezed lime is important, as it turns into a tangy frosting that will offset the sweetness of the sorbet.

- 2 large or 3 small mangoes
- 1 tub mango sorbet

- 2 limes, halved

Cut two thick slices lengthways from each mango as close to the stone as possible, so that you get the largest amount of flesh you can. Lay each slice skin-side down and make diagonal slashes across the flesh at 1cm intervals, down to (but not piercing) the skin. Do so again in the other direction to turn the slashes into diamonds.

Invert each slice so the diamonds of mango are spread out and wantonly calling you to suck them off. Serve each piece with a few scoops of mango sorbet and some lime to squeeze over the sorbet. Roll your sleeves up and fight as best you can over the remaining mango flesh.

PARTIES AND FEEDING A CROWD

Kate's birthday party (106)
Cottage pie with chorizo
Doughnut castle

A pudding party (109)
Birthday cake
Bellinis for all seasons

A Spanishy buffet (112)
Classic tapas
Chickpea and chorizo stew
Mum's cheesecake
Fresh chocolate orange turrón

Dom's Franglais feast (116)
Henry's unbelievably tender 18-hour beef, or roast rib of beef
Horseradish cream
Ed's roast potatoes
Pommes dauphinoise
The finest English cheese and biscuits
Les grands fromages

Good food to pick at with cocktails (120)
Chipolatas
A hunk of Parmesan and an ice pick
Mixed charcuterie
Olives, cornichons, caperberries
Toasted herby nuts

A hen night (123)
Thai crabcakes
Salt and chilli prawns
Mayonnaise
Manuela's ginger chicken
Roast seasonal vegetables
Katherine's strawberry shortbread

Bonfire night food (128)
Roast chestnuts
Baked Brie
Snobrød
Sausages on sticks
Baked bananas with rum and lime
Toasted marshmallows

Celebratory cocktails (132)
Ed's dark and stormy
Lychee martini
Classic margarita
Champagne cocktail

$\mathcal{P}$arties: love them or loathe them, you can't ignore them; they'll always be part of your life, and so they should be. You don't need an excuse to throw a party, the best ones often happen simply because it's Tuesday, or you've got a dose of spring fever, but special occasions are useful reminders that it's time for one. It's always good to acknowledge a moment which changes your life, whether it's the arrival of a new baby, or re-entry into the glorious world of singledom; it somehow helps it to feel real.

There's no question that being given a party is much more fun than giving one for yourself. It works in the round; you have to throw one for someone in order that another will do the same for you.

Decisions about how to celebrate get more complicated once you've grown out of the cardboard hat/entertainer/jelly kind of gathering. If you're not sure exactly what you want, the best way of deciding is to write out a list of options, and then a list of pros and cons by them. For example:

Type of party:	Pros:	Cons:
• Drinks party early	• Lots of people; lots of presents	• Canapés; complicated food; everyone leaves
• Dinner party	• Talk to everyone properly	• Limiting; could only involve best friends
• Eight-'til-late general invite party	• Fun; noisy; celebratory	• Hectic; no one turns up until eleven
• Party in a bar	• Glam; interesting venue possible	• Expensive; drinks party in disguise
• Activity party	• Original; bonding; hilarious	• Hard to be graceful/ sexy when red in the face and mud/ paint-smattered

Identify your strength and work to it. For some it may be cooking up a storm, for others dreaming up themes and costumes, compiling a great dancing playlist or making stupendous cocktails. Unless it's literally the party of your life, don't try and do everything – you'll lose your life to it for months in advance. In the end you need a great bunch of people, fun music, enough to eat and drink, and if possible, one memorable idea that sets it apart from other parties.

Romantic, kooky or trashy, volume is the key to creating a celebratory feeling, even if it's simply a dinner for eight people. Lots of flowers bring a room alive, so research a source that will make you a deal on volume and price – a friendly florist might do it for you, or you may find there's a market nearby. Lots of small posies everywhere with a couple of big bunches should do the trick. The same goes for lights; lots of small light sources, whether in the form of candles or strings of fairy lights, will have the greatest impact. Props always make a party swing, so consider a disco ball to hang in the middle of the room, some bunting, or feather boas for draping around cold shoulders. If you've got a few square metres in the corner of the room, it's not difficult or expensive to make a real disco. You can buy flashing lights that have a sensor that will react to the beat of the music, as well as a smoke machine, from any good high-street electrical store.

Be realistic about how much you can cope with yourself. Unless you've got willing friends who will reliably pitch in, a clump of people arriving at the same time could have you trying to play too many roles at once. Guests get grumpy if they don't get a drink fast enough, so ask around for people who can help – there's always someone who needs a bit of extra cash and it's not a bad way to earn it. If you don't know anyone, ask at local restaurants and bars for off-duty staff who may like some extra cash in hand. Otherwise, there are agencies who have trained waiting and bar staff. It feels glamorous to get professionals in; it also means there's someone else to manage logistics and, more importantly, to bring you a drink while you're getting ready.

By the way, don't feel you need to buy extra kit to cope with large numbers. Hiring is easy, surprisingly inexpensive and efficient. Most companies will even give you the option of sending everything back dirty, which cuts down on aftershock. You'll find hire companies on the internet and in the Yellow Pages.

The pudding party

A late drinks party is a good solution (in the city) if you want to invite lots of people without getting too bogged down by the expense and effort of feeding people a whole meal. It's also different, by virtue of which it is glamorous, without needing a budget to match the Oscars.

Nine o'clock is a good time to start – late enough that people have time to eat before, early enough that they won't give up and go to bed instead. One major advantage is that people tend to turn up on time, as opposed to the general eight-'til-late party, which for some reason people don't turn up to until the pubs shut. It's a good one particularly for grown-up birthdays since cake is then the only food you need to provide. It also means you can have one kind of booze – champagne if you're going the whole hog, but a dry cava or prosecco tarted up with some fresh fruit pulp (peach is the classic, pomegranate the prettiest) will go down equally well. The best bit of a late party is that you'll get a high tide of people who'll linger to talk properly as the party naturally thins. By the time the last person leaves, you'll be ready for bed, which seems like the right time for a party to end.

The theme party

Themed parties may not be cool, but they are fun. They're a good way of focusing your efforts and can also release you from having to spend a lot of money on catering. No one cares that they're not consuming vodka martinis and mini blinis

PS. The Catering Law of Diminishing Volumes
This is a handy trick to do with cooking in volumes that's worth knowing. It works like this: the more people you're feeding, the less they will eat. So, for every extra ten people, reduce the volume by twenty per cent. For eight people you'd cook the recipe as per instructions, but for eighteen to twenty people, you'd cook the recipe as for sixteen, and so on. Strange, but true.

when they're dressed like Limahl from Kajagoogoo. A theme can be inspired by a personal obsession (eighties tv heroes/Bollywood movies) or by an event (a big football match/last episode of a beloved tv series) and means sophistication can go hang as you unleash your kitschest fantasies on your home, your outfit, food and drinks.

I went to watch the France v England game with some friends during the last World Cup. It was a Sunday afternoon so they'd made a huge Franglais feast. There was a slow-roast rib of beef, with roast potatoes and pommes dauphinoise, a sloppy, stinking Brie and a stern hunk of Cheddar, good red wine and lots of cans of bitter. The English food was set up on one side of the room, the French on the other. We all ate it off our knees in front of the game on the television, chomping and shouting.

In the same spirit, trashy American programmes deserve trashy American food, a seventies movie demands cheese and pineapple on sticks, or, now that it never snows, make yourself a white Christmas party with only white food and drinks (vodka and milk, anyone?)

The hen party

Daisy gave the best one I've ever been to. There were only ten of us, and she'd bought matching leopard print kaftans from the market, and we were all given one to wear as we came in. It was a great leveller – all that potential sizing-up was extinguished immediately. There were glass fishbowls full of peonies, roses and lilies, which we all got to take home with us. She'd made us proper food (contrary to popular opinion, women love eating when left to their own devices) – plates of salty, spicy prawns and gently fiery crabcakes, followed by perfectly roast chicken with tangy ginger sauce. We ended up scoffing pudding – the crumbliest shortbread studded with strawberries and fixed by sweetened mascarpone – around the coffee table whilst reliving some of the less repeatable experiences of the past decade.

The centrepiece was a huge red leather-bound album to which we'd all contributed photos, notes and memories; a giant scrapbook that left most of us soaking in sentimental tears, curable (of course) only by the downing of more champagne. As a final flourish she'd made little goody bags with a photo of the bride and groom on one side and a copy of the engagement announcement on the other, filled with goodies. We had no need for limos, or male strippers, floating home in an alcoholic daze, heads filled with the joys of girl-friendship.

The activity party

It feels very 'jolly hockey sticks' to suggest parties that involve activities. Whether it's skating, bowling, go-karting or just a games night at home, the best thing about them is that you can do something really memorable without having to go into domestic goddess mode.

The key to making the party enticing is in how you approach the invitations. Don't go virtual, it's much more fun to receive something in the post. Apart from the practical information – where, when, what to wear – include some bits and bobs that will make people smile: a badge, an old-fashioned map, a colour-copied photograph of the activity with you or, if you're doing it for someone else, your guest of honour stuck on it, an entrance or bus ticket, 3-D glasses etc. The more creative you get, the more appealing the party is likely to be.

You don't necessarily have to take care of all the costs, but make sure your friends can afford the activity. Concentrate on contributing one element, like a picnic or the entry costs, which will go a long way to making people feel as though they are being invited to more than just a gathering. Make it clear what you are contributing and what your guests will have to cover.

The drinks party, if you must

To be honest, I loathe pre-dinner drinks. The room is always overheated and overpacked, there's never enough to eat, and just when you're beginning to enjoy the feeling of being dizzy with hunger, you get chucked out. But if you want or need to do one, make it classy by replacing beer and crisps with jugs of cocktails and more substantial eats.

Make up a few jugs of a cocktail beforehand, keeping ice in a separate bowl so that it won't melt and water it down. Keep the food simple by having plenty of two or three things rather than a little of many. Hit the deli counter with enthusiasm – smoked or salted nuts, olives, Japanese crackers, charcuterie, roll-mops, hard-boiled quails' eggs – the options are endless. Try to avoid too much fish – fishy breath beats even Marmite as a turn-off. When we were growing up, Noush used to chop up a whole salami and intersperse the slices with slivers of strong Cheddar on an old wooden board – it looked really pretty and was deliciously tangy, salty and rewarding to mop up booze.

Since party food seems to be stuck in a time warp anyway, relax into retro and roast a huge tray of chipolatas – you can never have too many. When I'm feeling generous, I like to buy a huge hunk of Parmesan and leave it on a board with an ice-pick for people to carve off in chunks. Tortilla (see page 162) is also excellently filling and easy to eat with fingers.

You could either spread a mixture of food and drinks on side tables around the room, or group each snack and cocktail in a different corner of the room to get people circulating in search of variety. Wooden chopping boards do a star turn here as large platters. If you've got anything greasy or sticky, tuck a few napkins underneath so people have got something to wipe their fingers on.

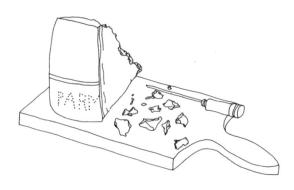

Bonfire night

Hot bottoms and frozen toes, everyone loves a bonfire. While fireworks night may be about the rush of light and noise that accompany the fireworks themselves, the heart of it is in the bright sparks and gold-red glow of the bonfire. It's the best way to bring out both the practicality in us (building it, lighting it) and the romance (wild nymph-like dancing, poetic gazing into its crackling heart).

However, any party, whatever the occasion and time of year, can incorporate a bonfire, and if you have the space, do. Conversely, if you are ever planning a bonfire, have a party to celebrate it. It's a central draw and the flickering light and surrounding darkness always create an amazingly magical and memorable atmosphere, as if the fire is the only light in the world, that you are the only people, and beyond the point where the fire's glow dims, there be dragons. Somehow, a party never ends until confidences are exchanged, kisses stolen, and the heat of the fire dies almost entirely.

As with barbecues, to use a bonfire for cooking, you need to protect your food from the flames. This could be either by building the bonfire on a base of big stones, which, as the flames die, are left incredibly hot and can be used for steaming (the New England clambake does this by strewing the stones with wet seaweed to produce steam); as a bread oven (think flatbread, pizza, naan); or more simply by wrapping the food in protective casing, like tin foil.

The surprise party

Even those who declare a deep horror generally turn out to be thrilled to find all their favourite people gathered in one place to celebrate with them, without having had to lift a finger. Get other friends involved – anyone loves being in on a secret, and sharing the load will make it much more fun to organize.

If you think people will dress up and your friend/lover/sister – or perhaps even victim – doesn't like being caught unprepared, invent some other reason to send him or her off for some grooming. Plan something quiet for the evening before to make sure they're not exhausted or hungover for the party. I say this with the resigned wisdom of having seen Ed going for it on December 30th two years in a row.

Kate's surprise thirtieth

Kate recently turned thirty, which means I, in turn, had to admit to more than that. In a loving sisterly way, Sam and I thought it would be amusing to torture her, by planning a surprise. There needed to be food, and dancing, and enough people, but not so many that it was a bun-fight. For the surprise to work, it needed to be on a night before her actual birthday.

We decided to transform my kitchen with a maypole of multi-coloured ribbons pinned into the centre of the ceiling and stretching out to the walls. We paced out the room and found we'd be able to squeeze forty people around the trestle tables we planned to hire. Pie, being a stuff of life, was the only answer for food; it's also easy to scale up to feed any number. Dressing up, we thought. Disco lights, a smoke machine, a great playlist, and dancing in the hall.

We made a proper invitation to post out because it's rare and rather exciting to get something friendly hitting the doormat in the morning. We scanned in a collage of pictures that we had printed onto a postcard to send to everyone, with a little badge pinned to the corner. We set up an email address for people to RSVP to. It dawned on me that in some ways, the planning was the most fun part.

I ordered five dozen Krispy Kreme donuts to stack into a tower and spike with sparklers instead of baking a cake. Sam fixed the decoy – that she was coming to take Kate out for a low-key sisters' dinner, and they'd come and fetch me from home on the way. Bottles of ketchup and Worcestershire sauce lay on each table with a couple of opened bottles of wine, posies of roses and peonies from the market. Everyone arrived on time. Giggling and whispering, they gathered behind the closed kitchen door. Kate and Sam arrived, and I opened the door, sure I had guilt written all over my face. We trudged upstairs to get my bag and ... SURPRISE!

Kate stood, blinking in the light, not quite able to believe her eyes. Given the situation, she was amazingly composed. Channelling the movie star within, she hugged everybody in turn, smiled, laughed and swung her hair. Cottage pie came out of the oven, peas from the pan, the final flourish of the sparkling doughnut tower into the darkened room. When Kate got up on the table to make a speech, you could see right up her miniskirt, which made us all laugh. We danced all night, to 'Thriller' and the like, or at least until the neighbours shut us down.

KATE'S BIRTHDAY PARTY
Feeds forty

Cottage pie with chorizo (and a porky trick with mince)

There is no one I wouldn't serve shepherd's or cottage pie to, and I've never come across a situation in which it would be unwelcome. The most important thing to keep in mind is that it needs to be extremely flavourful as it's always in danger of coming out quite bland under its potato hat. A surefire way of adding flavour is to include in the meat a couple of spicy sausages removed from their skins, or small cubes of pancetta fried at the beginning before the mince is added – I tend to use chorizo but any cured pork will help. Make sure you skim the fat off the meat before baking – there will be more than usual. This recipe will feed smaller numbers, too – simply divide all the ingredients appropriately, bearing in mind the Catering Law of Diminishing Volumes (see page 99). Serve with peas.

- 1.75kg chorizo (preferably the fresh cooking variety)
- 10 large onions, chopped
- 10 large carrots, finely chopped
- 5 celery sticks, chopped
- 30 garlic cloves, squashed under the blade of a knife
- about 200ml olive oil
- 3.5kg minced beef or lamb
- 10 tablespoons tomato purée
- 10 tablespoons ketchup
- 2 bottles red wine
- 2.5 litres chicken, beef or lamb stock

- 10 fresh bay leaves
- 2 large bunches thyme, finely chopped
- 1 teaspoon English mustard
- Worcestershire sauce
- Tabasco sauce
- salt and black pepper

for the topping
- 6kg floury potatoes, peeled
- 500ml milk
- 250g butter

If you are using fresh cooking chorizo, squeeze it out of its skin and break it up. Otherwise, chop the chorizo into small chunks.

In a stockpot or a couple of large casseroles, gently fry the chorizo until it colours and releases its oils. Add the onions, carrots, celery and garlic and fry until softened in the chorizo fat, adding as much of the olive oil as necessary.

Add the beef or lamb and cook, stirring, until it is thoroughly browned. Add the tomato purée, ketchup, wine, stock, herbs, English mustard, a dash of Worcestershire and Tabasco. Bring to the boil then reduce the heat to very low and simmer gently with the lid on for an hour if you've got it – if not, for 1/2 hour with the lid partially on. Remove the lid for the last 15 minutes of cooking, or until the mixture reduces to the right consistency.

Meanwhile, boil the potatoes for 40 minutes or until tender. You may need to do this in batches unless you have a huge number of saucepans. Drain and crush with a masher. Heat the milk until boiling and add it, along with the butter, to the potatoes. Mash energetically and season generously.

Preheat the oven to 180°C/gas 4. Skim the surplus fat off the meat mixture and check for seasoning – it may not need as much salt as usual as the chorizo is so highly spiced. I quite often add a good extra dash of Worcestershire, Tabasco and ketchup at this stage.

Divide the meat mixture between whatever dishes you are going to bake the pie in. I prefer to use several smaller ones (you'll need five or six) rather than a couple of large dishes, because it is then much easier and faster to serve. Top with the mash and bake for 45 minutes or until the top is golden and meaty gravy is bubbling up the sides.

Doughnut castle

Buy a doughnut and a half for each person – Krispy Kremes if you can find them (Google for stockists). Note: buying a variety is a mistake – the iced plain rings are always what everyone wants. Stack them into a high pyramid and speckle with candles or sparklers. Ta-da!

A PUDDING PARTY
Feeds ten

Birthday cake

I was in email chat with a friend in Scotland the other day, who was looking for a perfect birthday cake recipe. When I asked if the birthday cake needed to be chocolate, all I got in reply was several exclamation marks, so I took that to be a resounding yes. Here's mine, triply chocolaty. Serve with berries, and cream if you like, and a big glass bowl of Smarties to dip into.

for the cake
- 200g best dark chocolate
- 200g plain flour
- 50g cocoa powder
- 1 teaspoon baking powder
- $^1/_2$ teaspoon bicarbonate of soda
- pinch salt
- 200g unsalted butter, softened, plus extra for greasing
- 200g caster sugar
- 3 eggs
- 200ml milk

for the filling
- 50g best dark chocolate
- 25g cocoa powder
- 100g icing sugar
- 100g unsalted butter, softened

for the chocolate glaze
- 3 tablespoons apricot jam
- 25g unsalted butter
- 1 tablespoon cocoa powder
- 3 tablespoons icing sugar

to decorate
- crystallized violets, Smarties, or silver and gold hundreds and thousands

Preheat the oven to 180°C/gas 4. Butter two 20cm round sandwich tins and line with non-stick baking parchment. To make the cake: in a bowl over steaming water, melt half the chocolate. Chop the other half into small gravely pieces and set aside. Sift together the flour, cocoa, baking powder, bicarbonate of soda, and salt and set aside.

Cream together the butter and sugar until they are pale and light (an electric mixer is easiest for this). Add each egg in turn, beating well in between. Use a metal spoon to fold in both the melted and the chopped chocolate. Finally, fold in the flour and cocoa mixture a quarter at a time, alternating with a quarter of the milk, being careful not to force the air out.

When everything is combined, divide the batter between the tins and bake for 20–25 minutes. They are ready when a skewer inserted in the middle comes out easily – not clean necessarily, but without raw cake mixture on it. Remove from the oven and leave to stand for about ten minutes before turning the cakes out onto a wire rack to cool completely.

Now for the filling: melt the chocolate in a bowl over hot water. Sift together the cocoa and icing sugar. Cream the butter until light and fluffy. Add the cocoa and sugar mixture and beat well again for a few minutes. Fold in the melted chocolate, mixing well. When the cakes have cooled, cover the top of one generously with icing and sit the other on top to make a sandwich.

Finally, for the perfect shiny glaze: push the jam through a sieve, then melt it gently in a small saucepan. When it is runny, brush it over the top of the cake – this is to make the glaze stick.

Melt the butter over a low heat and stir in the cocoa, mixing until it is smooth. Add the icing sugar, spoonful by spoonful, blending until you have a mixture the consistency of heavy pouring cream. Spread immediately over the cake. You can smear it around the sides with a spatula if you like, or just allow it to drip down, which I think adds to the general effect.

Decorate straight away with what you will – crystallized violets, Smarties, silver and gold hundreds and thousands.

Spring bellini

This is really a buck's fizz. The blood oranges give it a wonderfully bright colour and zingy flavour.

- 2 blood oranges
- 1 bottle very cold prosecco

Squeeze the oranges and divide the juice between the glasses. Top up each glass with prosecco.

Summer bellini

This is the classic bellini, invented at Harry's Bar in Venice, and is made with the pulp of white peaches. You can now buy fresh fruit pulp vacuum-packed, which makes these drinks very easy, but in summer, it's worth buying white peaches to pulp yourself, as their delicate scent makes a glass of this sublime.

- 2 ripe white peaches, peeled, stoned and chopped
- 1 bottle very cold prosecco

Press the peach flesh through a sieve. Divide the pulp between champagne flutes. Top up each flute with prosecco.

Autumn bellini

Grab your apron for this – blackberry juice is extremely staining.

- 2 punnets blackberries
- 1 bottle very cold prosecco

Press the blackberries through a fine sieve, using a wooden spoon and being careful to catch the dark juice in the bowl underneath. Divide between the glasses and top up each glass with prosecco.

Winter bellini

I don't think much of the general fashion for pomegranate juice. I find the stuff that comes in cartons is syrupy and tastes of little but sugar. But this fresh juice is such a startling colour, and perks up a glass of very dry fizz.

- 3 pomegranates
- 1 bottle very cold prosecco

Squeeze the pomegranates as you might an orange – by cutting them in half and twisting over a juicer. Divide the ruby liquid between the glasses and top up each glass with prosecco.

A SPANISHY BUFFET
Feeds twenty-five

Classic tapas

I could hoover my way around Spain on tapas alone, and find the savouriness of the meat and cheese extremely good for accompanying pretty much any booze.

- thinly sliced serrano ham
- thinly sliced chorizo and salami
- thinly sliced manchego cheese with a pea-sized dot of quince jam (membrillo) on each
- olives, cornichons, caperberries
- squares of tortilla (see page 162)
- chunks of sourdough bread and saucers of olive oil

Lay out the tapas on trays or large plates. It's as simple as that.

Chickpea and chorizo stew

Brindisa Spanish deli in Exmouth Market makes this quick stew every lunch time throughout the winter, and you have to be early to get a portion – it's normally sold out by 1 o'clock. It's truly a one-pot wonder – at the deli, it's made in an electrically heated soup-maker as they have no stove. It couldn't be simpler or quicker, yet has the sort of depth of flavour that usually takes hours to achieve. This is my last-minute fallback in any situation, large or small (the recipe scales down easily). People love it because the flavours are intense and unusual. It's delicious with bread and a rocket, fennel and peeled cucumber salad. If you can't find any fresh cooking chorizo, substitute any good pork sausage plus four extra cloves of garlic and a tablespoon sweet smoked paprika.

- 1kg fresh cooking chorizo, cut diagonally into 3cm chunks
- 700g pancetta, roughly chopped
- 2 large red onions, roughly chopped
- 2 red bell peppers, deseeded and chopped
- olive oil
- 7 large garlic cloves, chopped
- 5 tablespoons dried oregano
- 1kg passata
- 7 x 400g cans chickpeas, drained, with 300ml of the water reserved
- 375ml white wine
- 500ml chicken stock or water
- 2 handfuls fresh flat-leafed parsley leaves, roughly chopped
- salt and black pepper

Fry the chorizo and pancetta in a large casserole over a fairly high heat until they begin to colour and release their oils. Remove with a slotted spoon and fry the onions and bell pepper in the meats' oils, adding a little extra olive oil if necessary, until golden and sweet.

Return the meat to the pan, turn the heat down, add the garlic and oregano and fry for a few more minutes. Add the passata, chickpeas, chickpea water, wine, stock and some salt and pepper. Bring to the boil and simmer for 20 minutes. (You can do this a day or two in advance if you like and gently reheat on the stove when the time comes.) Add roughly chopped parsley leaves to serve.

Mum's cheesecake

As far as I'm concerned, there's only one topping for cheesecake, and that's sour cream. It's how our Mum always made it. My only change is to make it with much less of the cream-cheese bit, because, to my mind, it's all about the biscuit base anyway. It becomes more of a tart than a cake, which is, I think, to its credit. To make this for just eight people, simply make one-third of the volume.

- 750g digestive biscuits
- 300g unsalted butter, plus extra for greasing
- 1.1kg cream cheese
- 375g caster sugar
- 6 large eggs

for the topping
- 600g sour cream
- 3 tablespoons caster sugar
- 1 teaspoon vanilla extract

Preheat the oven to 180°C/gas 4 and butter three 24cm spring-form tins.

Crush the digestive biscuits to a powder – either in a plastic bag with a rolling pin or, if you don't feel like exerting yourself, in the whizzer. Melt the butter and pour in the crushed biscuits, stirring until evenly distributed. Divide the mixture evenly between the tins, pressing it down firmly, and bake for 15 minutes.

Meanwhile, beat the cream cheese and caster sugar together in a bowl until soft, then add the eggs one at a time until the mixture is a smooth, heavy cream consistency. (You could do this in a food processor too.)

Pour the cream cheese mixture onto the cooked biscuit bases. Return them to the oven and bake for 15–20 minutes, until the cheesecakes are golden in patches on top, and very slightly wobbling in the middle. Allow them to cool completely in the tins.

Beat the topping ingredients together, then pour over the cheesecakes and chill for several hours before serving.

Fresh chocolate orange turrón

Turrón is a classic Spanish sweet, much like fresh marzipan, and is great served with coffee. You'll need a blender to make it.

- 500g blanched almonds
- 200g orange-flavoured dark chocolate, chopped
- 100g icing sugar
- pared zest of 1 unwaxed orange, cut into fine strips
- cocoa, for dusting

Line a baking sheet or tin with greaseproof paper.

Grind the blanched almonds in a blender or food processor until they are as fine as possible – this will take 4 or 5 minutes with it screaming full blast.

Add the chocolate, icing sugar and orange zest and whiz on until the chocolate is fully blended (you can see by the colour). It will probably ball up like pastry as it will get warm and soft from the heat of the blades, which is when you'll be done.

Spread the mixture out on the lined sheet so that it's about 1.5–2cm thick, then leave it to cool in the fridge. Cut into 2cm squares and dust with a little cocoa before serving.

DOM'S FRANGLAIS FEAST
Feeds ten to twelve

Henry's unbelievably tender 18-hour beef

Henry Dimbleby is one of the owners of Leon, the healthy fast-food chain that is making all the others pull their socks up. This slow-cook method makes the beef unbelievably tender, pink and juicy. Most importantly, it means you can go out on Saturday night, read the papers on Sunday morning, and still have a horde of people around for lunch. You will need an oven that can hold a low temperature very accurately, and a meat-thermometer probe.

- 2.25kg rib of beef
- wholegrain or Dijon mustard
- vegetable oil or dripping
- black pepper

Before you go out on Saturday night, set the oven temperature to 60°C (there is no precise gas mark equivalent of this), and check that it is stable by putting the meat probe in the oven and checking it after 10 minutes. You may need to adjust the temperature gauge a bit – a digital oven would make this much easier.

Slather the beef generously with mustard and black pepper. On the stove, heat a few tablespoons of oil or dripping in a roasting tray until very hot and brown the meat thoroughly on all sides – it should be as you'd like the finished product to look.

Stick the meat probe into the beef and put the joint in the oven so that you can see the gauge through the door. Before you go to bed, check the temperature on the probe – you needn't open the door. If it has already reached 50°C, the oven is running a bit hot, so turn it down accordingly.

Sleep well. In the morning, check the temperature every half an hour or so: 55°C will be rare, 60°C will be medium, 58°C will probably be about perfect. Once it hits that temperature (this should be about 1pm if you started the process at 8pm the night before), reduce the oven temperature to 58°C too and allow the meat to cook on for an hour – but there's no hurry, it will happily sit like that, getting juicier, for a few hours.

When you're ready to eat, remove the joint from the oven and carve it immediately – there's no need to rest it. There will be no juices for gravy, so if you want it, you'll have to make it from a previous stock, but the beef's so juicy you can just serve it with creamed horseradish.

Roast rib of beef

If you don't have a suitable oven, here's the regular method, too.

- 2.25kg rib of beef
- English mustard powder
- salt and black pepper

Preheat the oven to 230°C/gas 8. Make crosshatched scores across the top of the meat and rub with mustard powder, salt and pepper. Roast for 15 minutes to get the outside sizzling, then turn the oven temperature down to 170°C/gas 3 and roast for a further hour for rare and another 15 minutes for medium-rare. Allow the joint to rest for 15 minutes before carving.

Horseradish cream

Fresh creamed horseradish is a different creature to the bottled variety. It is worth buying a root whenever you come across one as you can store it in the freezer and simply peel as much as you need and grate from frozen.

- 100g fresh horseradish, peeled and finely grated
- 2 teaspoons sherry vinegar
- 1 teaspoon English mustard
- pinch sugar
- 150g crème fraîche
- pinch salt
- hint black pepper

Mix all the ingredients except the crème fraîche together in a bowl and let them sit and breathe with each other for a few minutes – it's a pretty powerful set of characters. Stir in the crème fraîche and eat within a couple of days.

Ed's roast potatoes

More often than not, I elbow Ed out of the kitchen, but he is king of the roast potato and I mess with that at my peril.

- vegetable oil
- 2 tablespoons goose fat or dripping (optional)
- sea salt
- 900g floury potatoes

Preheat the oven to 230°C/gas 8. Pour 1cm of vegetable oil into a roasting tin. Add the goose fat or dripping if you are using it, and scrunch over some good sea salt. Put it in the bottom of the oven to heat.

Peel the potatoes and cut them into the desired size – the larger the chunk, the longer they'll take. Put them in a large saucepan, bring to the boil in salted water, and cook for 7–8 minutes. Drain the potatoes in a colander, shaking and bashing them against the sides vigorously to give them a rough surface. You can encourage this by also scratching the surfaces with a fork.

When the oil in the oven is smoking hot, tip in the potatoes, turning to coat and return the tin to the oven. Roast for 1½ hours, turning occasionally so that the potatoes have even access to the oil. If you need to turn the oven down to accommodate roast meat, give them a fair blast for half an hour first, and then again at the end while the meat is resting. Eat immediately.

Pommes dauphinoise

Inspired by my friend Cat (though she shudders at the anchovies), this gratin is certainly inauthentic, but definitely winning. Making it a day in advance and reheating will do it no harm, and your sanity some good.

- 900g potatoes
- 450ml double cream
- 50ml milk
- 2 garlic cloves, finely chopped
- 2 sprigs thyme
- 1 bay leaf
- 4 anchovies, drained or rinsed of salt and chopped (optional)
- 20g butter
- sea salt and freshly ground pepper

Preheat the oven to 220°C/gas 7. Peel the potatoes and slice into 3mm rounds. Bring all the ingredients apart from the butter gently to a simmer in a large saucepan, and cook, partially covered, for 15 minutes, turning gently every so often without breaking the potatoes. Season to taste, remembering that the anchovies will bring with them their own salty hit.

Butter a shallow dish – earthenware for authenticity – and tip in the potatoes along with the heavy, scented juices, picking out the bay leaf, onion and thyme stalks. Smooth out the top and bake in the oven for 15–20 minutes until the top is golden and bubbling.

Alternatively, cover the unbaked dauphinoise and leave it somewhere cool for up to 24 hours before baking, in which case it will need 30 minutes in a medium oven.

The finest English cheese and biscuits

Isn't English cheese the best? While I'll conduct affairs with cheese from all over the world, it's to the ones made on these shores that I always return. You can buy excellent cheese by mail order or online if you don't have access to a good deli. Choose varieties such as:

- Montgomery's Cheddar
- Appleby's Cheshire
- Shorrock's Lancashire
- Harbourne Blue
- Innes Button
- Cornish Yarg
- Ticklemore

Les grands fromages

To be served with baguettes, or in true French style, with plenty of green salad:

- Brie aux truffes
- Epoisses affiné
- Saint-Marcellin
- Poiret de la Meause
- Vacherin du Mont d'Or
- Beaufort

Relish

GOOD FOOD TO PICK AT WITH COCKTAILS
Feeds as many as you like

Chipolatas

Allow at least 3 chipolatas per person. You can go for one variety or mix them up. Preheat the oven to 190°C/gas 5. Tuck the chipolatas snugly into a roasting tin just large enough to fit them in one layer and pour over enough water to come halfway up the sausages.

Roast for 20 minutes, turning a couple of times. The water will evaporate and they will be sticky and juicy. No need to prick them: you want them to cook internally in their juices, not to become greasy on the outside.

A hunk of Parmesan and an ice pick

Buy a large block of Parmesan in one piece, and put it on a board. Using an ice pick or a sharp knife, spear it around the edges to make large-ish shards of cheese that people can eat with their fingers. Leave the pick with the cheese so everyone can continue helping themselves.

Mixed charcuterie

Buy several different types of whole salami and put them on boards or plates. Slice off a good few slices of each to lay out, and leave the knife for people to cut their own slices afterwards.

Olives, cornichons, caperberries

Leave small bowls of olives, cornichons and caperberries, either separately or mixed together, near the charcuterie. They all work well together.

Toasted herby nuts

Natasha, my friend who lives in New York, always makes these to snack on with a drink. They are great to pick at, the scented warmth transforming them from an average bowl of nuts into a treat.

- 1 tablespoon olive oil
- 500g fresh nuts of your choice
- 1 tablespoon sea salt
- 4 tablespoons rosemary or thyme leaves

Over a fairly hot flame, heat the oil in a frying pan large enough to take the nuts in more or less a single layer. Empty the nuts into the pan and scatter over the salt and herbs.

Cook for 5 or so minutes, shaking the pan every so often to turn the nuts, until they are hot, golden and smell like the crackling heat of a Mediterranean summer (you'll know, even if you haven't been there).

A HEN NIGHT
Feeds ten

Thai crabcakes

You can add more or less chilli depending on how fiery you'd like these to taste. It's important to make sure you get rid of any wateriness in the crabmeat, and also that the oil is sizzling before you use it, otherwise the crabcakes won't get that all-important lightly crispy casing. They can be eaten hot or cold, or made in advance and gently reheated in a low oven.

- 250g fresh white crabmeat (or roughly chopped cooked prawns, but press out all the water you can if they're frozen)
- 150g fresh breadcrumbs
- 2 eggs
- 1 green chilli, minced
- 1 small red onion, minced
- 15g coriander leaves, finely chopped
- juice of 1 lime and grated zest of ¹/₂ lime
- vegetable or groundnut oil

Mix the crab, breadcrumbs, eggs, chilli, onion, coriander, lime juice and zest together with your hands. Dampen your hands with water and shape the mixture into 20 patties.

In a sauté pan, heat enough oil to cover the base by 1cm. When it's very hot, drop in a tiny bit of the mixture: it should sizzle enthusiastically. Fry the crabcakes, in batches if necessary (they need a little space as they cook), adding extra oil as needs be. They will want a couple of minutes on each side.

Set the cooked crabcakes aside on kitchen paper to absorb any excess grease. They can be served immediately, or at room temperature later.

Salt and chilli prawns

The salt-encrusted shell here keeps the flesh wonderfully juicy and sweet. If you can't find shell-on prawns, replace the large amount of salt with just a pinch, and fry even faster.

- 20–30 large uncooked North Atlantic prawns, shells and heads on (frozen and defrosted is fine)
- 1 tablespoon extra-virgin olive oil, plus extra for frying
- 3 tablespoons flaky sea salt, such as Maldon
- $1/2$ teaspoon chilli flakes or 2 dried bird's-eye chillies, crumbled
- mayonnaise (see below)

Wash the prawns thoroughly and pat dry. Toss with the olive oil in a bowl. Shake the salt and chilli out onto a plate and roll the prawns in it until they are coated. Heat a large frying pan – or wok – with the faintest spray of oil, until it's nearly smoking. Fry the prawns for a minute on each side and remove to a serving plate, to eat hot, or cold, with homemade mayonnaise.

Mayonnaise

Homemade mayonnaise is not difficult; you just need a beating arm with staying power. If your mayonnaise does begin to split, a teaspoon of tepid water and some robust beating might fix it. Otherwise, start with a single new egg yolk in a new bowl, and beat the old mixture into it very slowly. Then continue with oil, adjusting the volume as necessary.

If you would like your mayonnaise garlicky, add a crushed fat garlic clove at the beginning, along with the mustard and vinegar. If you'd just like a herby mayo – coriander would work well here, and parsley anytime – chop up a small handful of leaves and gently stir in at the end.

- 100ml extra-virgin olive oil
- 100ml vegetable oil
- 2 egg yolks
- 1 teaspoon Dijon mustard
- 1 teaspoon white wine vinegar
- pinch salt
- squeeze lemon juice

Combine the oils in a measuring jug, or something you can pour from slowly. Put the yolks in a medium-sized mixing bowl with the mustard, vinegar and salt and beat together with a whisk.

Add the oil very slowly, drip-by-drip to start with – it's only impatience that will cause your mayo to split, so hold your breath and keep going. Once you've added one-third of the oil agonizingly slowly, you can begin to speed up with a very slender stream of drips, beating constantly all the time. If the emulsion gets too thick, add a squeeze of lemon juice or a teaspoon of water to thin it. When the oil is absorbed, taste to check whether you'd like extra lemon juice.

Manuela's ginger chicken

Manuela is an amazing woman who looked after us when we were growing up. Somehow she managed to feed six constantly hungry children at bewilderingly different times of the day. This was the supper we most often clamoured for; each of us was ceremonially given the recipe when we left home.

- 2 medium-sized free-range chickens
- 4 spring onions, sliced into fine rounds
- 5cm fresh ginger, peeled and finely chopped
- 400g Philadelphia cream cheese
- 1 tablespoon ground ginger
- 1 tablespoon ground coriander
- olive oil
- sea salt and fresh black pepper

for the sauce
- 1 chicken stock cube
- squeeze lemon juice
- 2 teaspoons butter
- 2 garlic cloves, crushed
- 3 tablespoons ground coriander
- 2 teaspoons ground ginger
- 300ml double cream

Switch the oven on to 220°C/gas 7. Mash the spring onions and fresh ginger into the Philadelphia, and stuff into the cavities of the chickens.

Rub a little olive oil over the skin of the chicken, and dust with the ground ginger and coriander. Scatter over some sea salt and freshly ground pepper.

Roast the chickens for 20 minutes, then turn the oven temperature down to 190°C/gas 5 and continue cooking for a further 40 minutes.

Meanwhile, make the sauce. Dilute the stock cube with 3 tablespoons of boiling water from the kettle and add a squeeze of lemon. Melt the butter in a small saucepan and gently fry the crushed garlic cloves for a minute. Add the ground coriander and ground ginger and fry for another 30 seconds or so, then pour in the chicken stock. Cook, whisking, for another minute so that the mixture becomes a paste.

Turn the heat under the saucepan right down and add the cream, still whisking, until all is combined. Cook for 3 or so minutes, then taste.

When the chickens are done, allow them to rest for 15 minutes before carving. Serve the sauce in a bowl on the side and spoon out the stuffing to eat alongside.

Roast beetroot and butternut (for winter)

If the beetroot are small, young and plump you can leave them whole. If you are cooking them alongside the chicken, roast everything at 190°C/gas 5 rather than starting higher and turning the oven down. Alternatively, you can make the beetroot and butternut squash in advance and pile them up high on a serving plate to be eaten later at room temperature.

- 10 medium beetroot, or 15 small ones
- 1 butternut squash
- olive oil
- 2 sprigs thyme
- balsamic or sherry vinegar (optional)
- sea salt

Wash, top and tail the beetroot and cut into 3cm cubes. Top and tail the butternut squash, split it open and remove all the seeds, then cut it into 3cm cubes too.

In a roasting dish large enough to hold the vegetables in more or less one layer, toss them with a few tablespoons of olive oil, a generous scrunch of sea salt and the thyme.

Roast along with the chicken if you have a big enough oven – if the vegetables seem like they're cooking too fast, remove them after 45 minutes and finish at 180°C/gas 4 while the chicken is resting.

Otherwise, roast in advance for 1 hour at 180°C/gas 4, then serve them at room temperature, tossed with a drizzle of balsamic or sherry vinegar.

Roast fennel and cherry tomatoes (for summer)

Like the beetroot and butternut recipe opposite, this can be prepared in advance and served at room temperature, or cooked alongside the chicken.

- 3 bulbs fennel
- olive oil

- 500g cherry tomatoes on the vine
- sea salt

Preheat the oven to 180°C/gas 4. Chop the fennel vertically into quarters and then again into eighths, so that the pieces hold together at the root. Put them in a roasting dish with some olive oil, tossing gently to coat, and scrunch over the sea salt.

Roast the fennel for 15 minutes, turn, and roast for another 15 minutes. Add a mug of water to the roasting dish and lay the tomatoes over the top, still on the vine. Drizzle a little more olive oil over them and continue cooking for 30 minutes.

Katherine's strawberry shortbread

This is a different shortbread – it is crumblier and lighter than the biscuits on page 141 – but you could use that recipe for the base, too, if you prefer.

- 225g self-raising flour
- 75g plain flour
- 225g butter
- 3 tablespoons demerara sugar

- 250g mascarpone
- icing sugar, sifted
- 1 large punnet strawberries, hulled but left whole

Put the flours in a mixing bowl and rub in the butter, or whiz in a processor until evenly distributed. Lightly stir in the sugar (it must be demerara, for the crunch), or pulse in the processor until the pastry just comes together. Shape the pastry into a flat disc and chill for half an hour.

Preheat the oven to 180°C/gas 4. Press the pastry evenly into the base of a 28cm spring-form tin and bake for 12–15 minutes until it takes on a pale gold shortbread appearance. Remove from the oven and allow to cool for a few minutes in the tin before removing the sides. Let it cool for at least an hour.

Beat the mascarpone with a little sifted icing sugar to taste. Just before you want to eat it, spread the mascarpone over the pastry and stud with the strawberries. Dust with more sifted icing sugar.

BONFIRE NIGHT FOOD
Feeds twelve

Roast chestnuts

You want to allow a handful of chestnuts per person, bearing in mind that you might get the occasional dodgy one. About 60 would probably be right.

Make a slash in the skin of each chestnut, apart from one. Put them on a shovel and place in the embers of the fire. When you hear the skin of the unslashed one burst open, the rest will be ready to eat.

Baked Brie

Given its size, Brie is good for feeding a crowd, but you could substitute with any soft cheese like Camembert or Vacherin.

- 1 whole Brie cheese
- 2–3 sprigs thyme
- snobrød or breadsticks

Tear a hole in the middle of the top of the Brie and tuck in the thyme. Wrap the whole cheese in foil and lay in the hot ashes towards the outer edge of the fire, where the heat's not too intense. Bake for 10–15 minutes, spinning the cheese every so often so that it's equally exposed to the heat.

To eat, cut around the top of the rind in a circle and peel it back like a lid. To eat, dip breadsticks, or much better, snobrød, into its melting mass.

Snobrød

The first time I had this was when a Danish friend made it at a summer party. She brought out a basin of bread dough, and we all took a small ball of it, which we flattened out into a ribbon shape and wound around twigs to poke into the edge of the fire. We all sat holding our bread twigs in the fire like fisherman, and were amazed and delighted by how delicious the bread was, slightly scalded and ashy on the outside and fresh and light within. The important thing is to include enough oil so that the bread doesn't stick to the wood.

- 35g fresh yeast (or 20g fast-action dried yeast)
- 600ml lukewarm water
- 2 tablespoons salt
- 75ml grapeseed oil
- 750g strong white flour, plus extra for dusting

If using fresh yeast, mix it in a measuring jug with the lukewarm water and leave to activate for a few minutes (you will see it come alive), then add the salt and oil. If you're using dried yeast, mix it straight into the flour and just add the salt and oil to the warm water.

Put the flour in a bowl big enough to take all the ingredients and get both your hands into. Pour in the liquid a little at a time, squelching and rubbing it into the flour as you go, until it becomes a malleable but not too sticky dough – you may need a little extra flour or water.

Knead well for 10 minutes on a floured surface. This is extremely good for upper-body toning, so don't dally (it's also necessary for the bread). The dough will become smooth and elastic after a while. Leave it somewhere warm, covered, to rise for at least an hour, then knock it back and knead again before dividing it into golf-ball sized balls.

Send kids or annoying people off to find a long stick for each person and pare off 15cm of bark at one end of each of them. Stretch the balls of dough out into long snakes about 1cm wide and wrap around the sticks where the bark has been removed.

Hold the dough deep in a glowing corner of the fire rather than right in the flames, turning as it cooks. It will take about 5 minutes depending on how hot your fire is. The snobrød is ready when you can pull it off the stick.

Peel the bread off and eat as it is, or dip into melting cheese. Or, for something really sickly, instead of peeling it off in a string, wiggle it off to give a bread cup and pour golden syrup into the cavity – quite disgusting unless you've got a really sweet tooth, but kids love it.

Sausages on sticks

Sticks are a great way to cook sausages. I find it best to thrust the stick right up vertically through the sausage, and again, cook over coal and embers rather than flames. Allow 7–10 minutes of turning over the fire before trying one, which is the only way to figure out if they're cooked, and half the fun anyway. Expect them to look like they've been through the Normandy landings by the time you actually get to eat them.

Baked bananas with rum and lime

I've never worked out why it's so exciting to bake a banana in a fire when I'd never do it in the oven – perhaps it's something to do with reliving childhood. In any case, they are delicious, either parcelled up like this, with a little rum, brown sugar and lime, or for something totally trashy, you can also try splitting them lengthways and stuffing them with chocolate and marshmallows. This recipe feeds six, and you will need six 30cm square sheets of foil.

- 6 bananas
- 3 tablespoons rum
- juice of 2 limes
- 2 teaspoons muscovado sugar

Peel the bananas and cut them diagonally into slices about 2cm thick. Toss with the rum, lime juice and sugar, and divide between the sheets of foil.

Fold the foil into firm packages, sealing well, and grill over low–medium coals for 15–20 minutes.

Toasted marshmallows

Never underestimate the pink and white pleasures of a molten marshmallow. Spear each marshmallow with a long twig and roast over glowing embers until they're starting to blacken on the outside. Try to resist eating for at least 20 seconds after you've removed them from the heat, so that they are a manageable temperature.

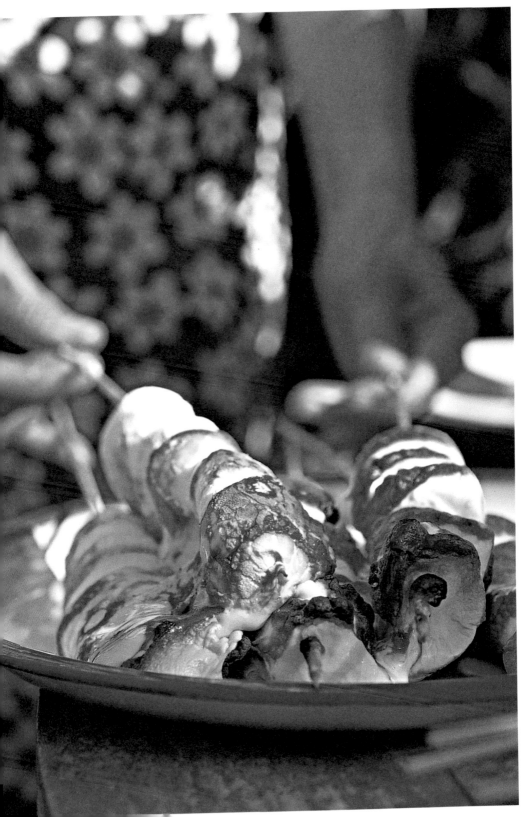

CELEBRATORY COCKTAILS

Ed's dark and stormy

If you'd prefer a mojito, simply replace the dark rum with white rum, and the ginger ale with soda.

- 1–2 limes per person, quartered
- small handful mint per person
- 1 tablespoon demerara sugar per person (or to taste)
- 1 part dark rum
- 2 parts ginger ale
- ice

In a large jug, pound the limes, the mint and the sugar with the handle of a rolling pin until well bashed. Add the rum. You can allow this mixture to steep for several hours in the fridge.

When you are ready to drink, top with ginger ale and add extra sugar to taste, if necessary. Serve over ice with a straw to suck up the crunchy sugar.

Lychee martini

If you can find a tin of lychees, drop one of the fruits into the bottom of each glass.

- 2 parts vodka
- 1 part lychee juice
- $^1/_2$ part dry vermouth
- ice

Put the glasses into the freezer for at least 10 minutes before serving. Stir the ingredients together over ice, then strain into the frozen glasses.

Classic margarita

Natasha always makes frozen margaritas when you stay for the weekend. That first mouthful of tangy, boozy, sludgy ice always spells good times to me.

- 1 lime, halved
- fine salt
- 2 parts tequila
- 1 part Cointreau or triple sec
- 1 part lime juice
- ice

Rub the cut lime around the rim of the glasses. Tradition calls for a martini glass, if you have one. Put a good layer of fine salt into a saucer and turn the rims of the glasses in it.

Shake the tequila, Cointreau (or triple sec) and lime juice together over ice, then strain into the salted glasses.

For a frozen margarita, half-fill a blender with ice and pour in the alcohol until it reaches the same level. Blend furiously until fine then divide between glasses – again, salted if you like.

Champagne cocktail

I'm no longer sure whether Champagne cocktails are classy or naff, but I do know that they make fun drunks. Cognac is the classic spirit to use, but Cointreau is a great twist, too.

- 1 white sugar cube per glass
- Angostura bitters
- 1 tablespoon cognac or Cointreau per glass
- Champagne

Drop a sugar cube into the bottom of a Champagne flute and cover with 2 dashes of bitter. Add the cognac or Cointreau and top with cold Champagne. The cube will last a few rounds so you can simply top up with Champagne.

COOKING FOR COMFORT

Growing up but not quite there yet (139)
Spinach and Gruyère quiche
Tommi's rhubarb and Pernod compote
Shortbread

On the mend, but still suffering (142)
Sausagemeat and cabbage casserole
Better bread and custard pudding

A supper to yank you from the depths (145)
Chicken noodle soup
Rosewater rice pudding

For new parents who still feel like kids underneath (147)
Manuela's chicken and tarragon pie
Caramel apples

Sustenance for shaken movers (150)
Steak sandwiches
World-beating flapjacks
Goo-goo cake

Sometimes all you want is a fairy godmother to appear on your doorstep bearing a steaming pie, a batch of brownies and a bottle of red wine. At others, you have to be the fairy. Cooking for friends in need is very different to entertaining. It's about strapping on your wings and sprinkling a bit of magic dust into a difficult situation. It's about your time rather than your money, and it's wholly unselfish apart from the halo-glow you flit around in for the day (which you might want to keep under wraps).

Comfort food means childhood and home, and everyone has their own idea of it. Depending on who you ask, this may be foie gras or Findus crispy pancakes. To some it's doughy stodge, to others, puréed vegetables. To me it means the sausagemeat wrapped in cabbage we often ate on school nights, roast chicken with crunchy gingered skin, and hazelnut Ski yoghurts.

Complex flavours and unusual textures simply won't do. You'll want your savoury dishes to taste clean and true, and the sweet ones to be loaded with sugar and fat. There's no room to mess around with food fashion here; your body simply won't be denied the comfort it seeks.

There's no question that troubled times often call for ordering in. If you're going to provide a takeaway service, you've got to be practical about what food to make, and what pot or container to make it in. It's helpful if it can be frozen, even better if it can go straight into the oven or on top of the stove. Steer in the direction of one-pot wonders, such as pies, which don't need much accessorizing.

As in most culinary situations, if you don't have the time, energy or will to make something right from scratch, shopping well gets you a long way. Seeking out something special – a certain leaf tea, a beloved scented nougat – can mean just as much, but there are definitely different kinds of food that suit different states of mind.

Life-changing moments call for comfort food

There are pivotal moments in life when it seems to me that only food can comfort and tether: when your heart is broken, when you become a new parent, and when you move house. These situations change the landscape of your life so completely that only the very gentlest of sustenance will sooth and stabilize you.

Sod's Law dictates that when you're at your lowest, the world will be at its most brutal: the sun won't shine, you'll be overdrawn, canoodling couples will display unwarranted levels of affection in public while new mums with pushchairs squeeze you off the pavement. I remember clearly my own hard landing, on returning home to live after three years in America. I was heartbroken after a doomed love affair, and it was January, a brutal month to arrive back: nothing blooming, not even snowdrops, the parks grey mud and the trees twiggy. Everyone was on a diet, I had no job and nothing to do but sit smoking and surrounded by boxes, waiting in a self-pitying way for someone to call.

At times such as these, I found chicken soup and chocolate ice cream to have the strongest pair of arms. They don't need chewing, and provide that necessary shot of savoury warmth, followed by the icy oblivion best found in the bottom of a round cardboard tub.

A different sort of desperation entirely, but new parents need looking after too. You'll need to take the food to them as they will rarely leave their home, for the first few weeks at least. Their days will disappear under the combination of unfamiliar tasks and no sleep and an endless stream of visitors to cater for, so all food will be welcomed at all times. When they're most in need of straightforward nourishment, good food is in danger of falling off the list of important things in favour of ready meals and pizza delivery.

It's most useful to think of food that can be eaten once hot, leaving delicious leftovers in the fridge for the following day. Pies are brilliant as they can be eaten with one hand, and have the bonus of being able to convey a message in pastry on the top, (like the name of the new baby). New mums will also appreciate presents made up of the same food they were told to avoid during pregnancy, such as runny cheese.

Moving house is hungry work. Each room squirrels away the individual moments that make up our lives; packing them up is physically and emotionally draining, and a friendly face bearing edible gifts will go a long way to filling the empty space left behind. I'm absurdly attached to my home; it's seen me through some troubled times. The very idea of moving fills me with such misery that I daren't contemplate it. When it happens, and it will, Ed will have to hire a digger to extract me from it. I already have to be winkled out for lunch or supper, and can spend days mooching around without noticing that I haven't stepped out of the door.

The key to helping people when they're moving house is not to expect them to have access to anything – perhaps not even a kettle. If you want to bring food it needs to be practical – sandwiches are probably the most sensible option, and you don't have to make them yourself. Relatively wholesome biscuits and chocolate are always welcome, but if you really want to worm your way into their hearts forever, buy two new mugs, a packet of teabags, milk, and sugar – and take your kettle with you.

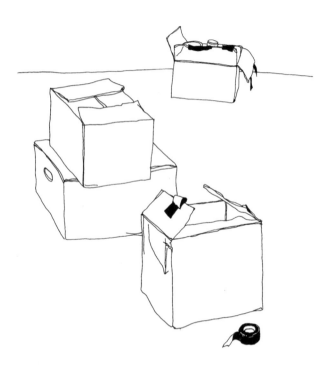

GROWING UP BUT NOT QUITE THERE YET
Feeds six

Spinach and Gruyère quiche

It would be more fashionable to call this a tart – and it's certainly beautiful enough in looks, taste and texture – but when push comes to shove, I can't bring myself to. A quiche is a quiche is a quiche. The success of this one depends on all the liquid being squeezed from the cooked spinach, otherwise it won't set.

- 375g ready-made shortcrust pastry
- 1kg spinach, washed
- 150ml double cream
- 4 medium eggs
- freshly grated nutmeg

- 150g Gruyère cheese, grated
- 150g cherry tomatoes, halved
- groundnut oil
- sea salt and black pepper

First make your pastry case. Preheat the oven to 190°C/gas 5. Grease a loose-bottomed, high-sided 23cm tart tin. Roll out the pastry until it is 5mm thick and press into the tin, trimming off all but a little extra pastry from around the top, as it probably will shrink a bit.

Prick the bottom with a fork, lay over a sheet of baking parchment and fill with a layer of baking beans. Bake for 10 minutes, then remove the parchment and beans and return the pastry case to the oven for a further 15 minutes. It should turn a pale biscuity colour. Remove from the oven and set aside to cool.

Now for the filling: place the spinach in a large saucepan with just the water that clings to the leaves after washing. Cover and cook over a medium heat for 5 minutes, stirring it halfway through, so that it collapses (you may need to do this in two batches).

Drain the spinach in a sieve and press out as much liquid as possible. Then turn it out onto kitchen paper and squeeze out even more liquid before chopping the spinach roughly.

In a mixing bowl, whisk together the cream, eggs, plenty of salt and pepper and a grating of nutmeg. Stir in the spinach, making sure it is evenly distributed. Add half the Gruyère and more salt and pepper to taste if necessary. Transfer the mixture to the pastry case and smooth over the surface.

Toss the tomatoes in a bowl with just enough oil to coat them, and season. Scatter them over the surface of the tart and press them into the filling so that they are level with the spinach. Sprinkle over the remaining cheese and bake for 35–40 minutes, until the quiche is golden on the surface and just set.

Leave the quiche to cool for 10 minutes before serving with salad. It is best eaten warm from the oven, but will also reheat with reasonable success.

Tommi's rhubarb and Pernod compote

Thomasina Miers is one of the most instinctive, unusual cooks I know. The Pernod here is an inspired partner to the rhubarb. Serve with softly whipped cream, crème fraîche or Greek yoghurt.

* 125–200g sugar, depending on taste
* 450–600g rhubarb (about 6–8 stems), cut into 2.5cm pieces
* ¹/₂ vanilla pod, split lengthways
* juice and finely grated zest of 1 unwaxed orange

* 1 tablespoon Pernod

to serve
* 250g whipped cream, crème fraîche or Greek yoghurt

In a saucepan, melt the sugar with 25ml of water. Add the rhubarb, vanilla pod and orange juice and zest. Cover and simmer gently for 15 minutes, then remove the lid and simmer a little faster for another 10 minutes. Set aside to cool.

When cool enough to handle, scrape the seeds from the vanilla pod into the fruit. Add the Pernod and blend or whisk until the mixture is fairly smooth. Taste for sweetness before serving, adding more sugar if necessary – rhubarb can taste very different depending on the time of the season.

Shortbread

This recipe is easy to remember as the volumes go 1-2-3. You can roll it out thicker, for a stodgier biscuit (particularly good at tea time) but you'll need to cook it for a few minutes longer. To vary the shortbread, you can flavour it by adding the finely grated zest of an unwaxed orange or lemon, or some crushed unsprayed rose petals or lavender flowers, when you add the flour.

- 100g caster sugar
- 200g butter
- 300g plain white flour
- pinch salt

Cream the sugar and butter together. Sieve the flour and salt together, and mix into the butter mixture to make a soft dough, being careful not to overwork it.

Wrap the dough in clingfilm and allow to rest in the fridge for 1 hour, then leave it for half an hour at room temperature before you roll it out.

Preheat the oven to 170°C/gas 3. Roll the dough out to a thickness of 5mm and cut into whatever shapes you like – cookies, crescents, or just fingers (I find this can be very difficult as the dough is so crumbly it breaks up, so I often end up with the strange, rough-edged shapes that it naturally breaks into, and I've decided to like them).

Line a baking sheet with parchment paper and place the biscuits on it. Bake for 15–20 minutes, or until golden. Remove from the oven and after 5 minutes, carefully lift the shortbread onto a rack. They will still be a bit soft but will turn crisp as they cool.

ON THE MEND, BUT STILL SUFFERING
Feeds four

Sausagemeat and cabbage casserole

It's important here to discard the sausage skins, as the parcels should be so melting that they can be eaten with a spoon. Good served with smooth, buttery mash.

- 8 excellent pork sausages, herby ones if you like
- 8 large cabbage leaves
- 50g pancetta, cubed, or streaky bacon, chopped
- 1 carrot, finely chopped
- 1 celery stick, finely chopped
- 1 small onion, finely chopped
- olive oil
- 600ml chicken stock
- 1/2 x 400g tin chopped tomatoes, drained of their juice (or 2 fairly large fresh tomatoes, skinned, deseeded and chopped)
- 1 x 400g tin haricot beans

Squeeze the sausagemeat from its skins and set aside. In a large pot of boiling water, blanch the cabbage leaves for 4–5 minutes or until they go floppy. Remove, refresh in cold water and pat dry.

Fry the pancetta, carrot, celery and onion in a little oil, stirring occasionally, until the meat colours and the vegetables soften and begin to turn golden.

Meanwhile, gently but firmly wrap the sausages in the cabbage leaves and 'fasten' with a toothpick or two. Place in a small casserole that fits them snugly. Add the pancetta and vegetable mixture, stock and tomatoes. Bring to the boil, then reduce the heat to a murmur and cook, partially covered, for 25 minutes. Turn the parcels carefully from time to time if they are rising above the soupy broth.

Five minutes before they are ready, drain the beans and press them into the thickening liquid. Allow them to heat through for a few minutes. Carefully remove the toothpicks, and taste for seasoning before serving.

Better bread and custard pudding

This has got about as much to do with the soggy eggy curranty bread-and-butter pudding as my elbow. It is much closer to a fine, slightly caramelized crème anglaise (sorry to be pretentious), and would take to brioche as well as, if not better than, plain old bread. You can, of course, add sultanas if you're attached to them, but soak them in the booze first. Compose the pudding in advance if it helps your schedule, allowing it to sit and soak overnight if you like.

- a little butter
- 6 slices day-old white bread
- 150ml milk
- 150ml sour cream or crème fraîche
- 75ml condensed milk
- 2 egg yolks

- 1 teaspoon vanilla extract (or seeds scraped from $1/2$ vanilla pod)
- 50ml dark rum, whisky or brandy (optional)
- 2 tablespoons dark muscovado sugar

Butter a shallow baking dish. Cut the crusts off the bread and cut each slice into four triangles. Arrange half in a single layer in the baking dish, setting the rest aside.

Beat together the milk, sour cream, condensed milk, egg yolks, vanilla and booze, if using, and pour half of the mixture over the layer of bread. Turn each slice over so it can soak up the rich juice, and arrange in a vaguely pretty or at least even pattern.

Add another layer of bread and pour the rest of the egg mixture over it. Fidget again with the slices so that they are as covered as possible – there should be bits sticking out above the liquid, which will turn golden and chewy.

Crumble the muscovado sugar over as finely as possible – you'll need to do this with your fingers. This is the point where you can allow it to sit and soak for a while.

Preheat the oven to 180°C/gas 4 and bake for 15–20 minutes – if the top hasn't browned at all, give it a quick blast under the grill. Eat immediately, with cream, crème fraîche or ice cream if you like.

A SUPPER TO YANK YOU FROM THE DEPTHS
Feeds four

Chicken noodle soup

Someone once told me that an American research institute had proved that chicken soup actually had mending properties. When we were little, chicken noodle soup came in granules which were reconstituted for us patients recovering from chickenpox or measles. Now I try to keep a pot of the real thing on my stove throughout the winter. I can't say whether it actually keeps colds away, but it's very good at preventing me from eating chocolate on a gloomy afternoon.

The following isn't so much a recipe as a guideline – depending on my mood, I'll take it in different directions: to the Mediterranean with thyme, lemon juice and olive oil, or Southeast Asia with lime, nam pla, soy sauce and chilli. But the Jewish granny in me likes it most plain with noodles.

for the broth
- 1 free-range chicken, plus extra wings, drumsticks or carcass if you have any
- 3 carrots
- 2 celery sticks
- 2 onions, peeled and halved
- 2 bay leaves
- parsley stalks, fennel, leek tops, if you have them
- 1 teaspoon whole black peppercorns

to serve
- 75g spaghetti, broken up, or macaroni
- chopped carrot, leek, fennel, etc., (optional)

Fit all the ingredients snugly into a casserole. Cover with water and bring slowly to the boil, skimming away any greyish scum regularly. As it begins to boil, reduce the heat to a very gentle simmer and cook, partially covered, for 1 hour.

Take out the whole chicken, remove the breasts and set aside. Discard any skin that's easy to pull off. Return the chicken to the pot and continue simmering for at least 45 minutes, but the longer the better.

Before eating the soup for the first time, allow it to cool. The broth should jellify and the fat turn opaque on the surface, so that you can gently scrape it off with a spoon (this is easiest after a night in the fridge). The pot can then stay on top of the stove, being reheated and topped up with a little water whenever necessary, as long as it's brought fully to the boil each day.

To eat, remove some of the broth to a smaller pan, add the pasta along with some more vegetables if you like, and cook until the pasta is done and the vegetables soft. Shred the chicken breasts to whatever size you like, divide between bowls and cover with the steaming broth and vegetables, remembering to top up the main pot with extra water.

Rosewater rice pudding

This scented mass is both comforting and distinctive. The risotto method adds richness, which means you need no cream. It can be eaten tepid or cold.

- 30g unsalted butter
- 100g risotto or pudding rice
- 150ml pudding wine
- 1.2 litres full-fat milk
- 150g sugar
- pinch salt

- 15 cardamom pods, seeds pounded and husks picked out
- 4 tablespoons rosewater
- 75g unsalted pistachio nuts, peeled and roughly crushed

Preheat the oven to 150°C/gas 2. On the stove, melt the butter in a casserole over a medium heat, add the rice and stir until coated and translucent.

Add the pudding wine and allow to bubble and reduce for a couple of minutes. Then pour in 1 litre of the milk, plus the sugar, salt and ground cardamom. Stir to combine thoroughly and bring to a gentle simmer.

Cover the casserole and transfer to the oven for 60–75 minutes, checking and stirring every half an hour. If all the milk has been absorbed before the rice is completely tender, you may need to top it up with the milk you have set aside.

When done, remove the pudding from the oven and allow to cool a little before stirring in the rosewater. Serve warm or cool with the crushed pistachio nuts on top.

FOR NEW PARENTS WHO STILL FEEL LIKE KIDS UNDERNEATH
Feeds six

Manuela's chicken and tarragon pie

I love pie – it can meet any occasion, from formal to deeply comforting. You can make the filling up to two days in advance, then cover and refrigerate or freeze.

- 1 free-range chicken
- 2 tablespoons dried tarragon
- 75g butter
- 4 heaped tablespoons plain flour
- 4 sprigs fresh tarragon

- 600ml milk
- 375g ready-made puff pastry
- 1 egg, beaten
- sea salt and black pepper

Preheat the oven to 220°C/gas 7. Wash the chicken, pat dry and sprinkle the dried tarragon over the skin, along with some salt and pepper. Roast for 45 minutes, so that it is still undercooked. Set aside until cool enough to handle.

Meanwhile, make a béchamel sauce. Melt the butter over a medium heat then add the flour and, stirring all the while, cook for about 5 minutes, until you have a golden, sandy roux. Put two sprigs of fresh tarragon into a separate saucepan with the milk and warm through without letting it boil.

Add the hot milk slowly to the roux, stirring to incorporate it fully. Continue cooking at a gentle simmer until the sauce is smooth and has the consistency of double cream. Pick the leaves from the remaining tarragon sprigs and add to the sauce. Season to taste with salt and pepper and remove the sauce from the heat.

Discard the skin of the chicken. Remove all the flesh from the carcass in whatever shape you prefer – either shreds or chunks. Set a small jug of the sauce aside to serve as gravy, and mix the rest with the chicken. Decant the filling into your pie dish. You can leave this mixture in the fridge for a couple of days or even freeze it for later use.

When you are ready to bake your pie, preheat the oven to 220°C/gas 7. Roll out the pastry until it is 5mm thick and drape over the dish, allowing a generous lip. Brush with the beaten egg. Fashion any excess pastry into shapes to decorate the pie – letters to spell a word, leaves are pretty too – and brush again with the egg.

Bake the pie for 30–40 minutes, or until the pastry is puffed up and golden. Serve with extra tarragon sauce, warmed gently, on the side.

Caramel apples

These really are sweet, but could be made with cooking apples for a pucker to contrast with the sauce. You can do all this a little in advance if you like and let it sit at room temperature until you're ready to eat – the golden syrup will prevent the sauce becoming hard or granuley.

- 100g unsalted butter
- 100g muscovado sugar
- 5 heaped tablespoons golden syrup
- 6 small apples, peeled, cored, quartered then halved again
- vanilla ice cream

Melt the butter, sugar and golden syrup in a saucepan over a medium heat for 2–3 minutes, stirring until the butter is melted and the sugar dissolved.

Add the apples and cook for 3–5 minutes until the apple is just tender. Reduce the heat and simmer for 2 minutes so that the sauce is thick and syrupy.

Gently warm through again when you're ready to eat and serve them with the ice cream.

SUSTENANCE FOR SHAKEN MOVERS
Feeds four

Steak sandwiches

This marinade, modelled on a classic South American steak sauce, has got real punch. If it's too strong for you, rein back on the garlic and chilli.

- 1 avocado, peeled and stoned
- 4 x 150g minute steaks, as wild as possible
- 2 baguettes (or 8 slices very fresh sourdough bread)
- peppery salad leaves

for the marinade
- 3 tablespoons chopped flat-leafed parsley
- 2 tablespoons chopped fresh oregano
- 2 tablespoons red wine vinegar
- 2 tablespoons lemon juice
- 1 red chilli, finely chopped
- 2 garlic cloves, pounded until smooth
- 1 teaspoon ground cumin
- 1 teaspoon hot smoked paprika
- 120ml olive oil
- sea salt and black pepper

Whiz or pound together thoroughly all the ingredients for the marinade. Set aside 2 dessertspoons of the spice mixture and use the remainder to marinate the steaks for 1–24 hours.

When almost ready to cook, mash the reserved marinade into the avocado. Fry your steaks over a high heat for a minute or two on each side.

If you're eating them immediately, put the steaks into the bread, push in the avocado mixture, and stuff in some peppery salad leaves for good measure. If you're making them for a later picnic, allow the meat to cool a little before compiling the sandwiches.

World-beating flapjacks

This will make enough for a small roasting tin, so you can keep some back for tea, too. They will store in a tin for a week (if they last that long).

- 250g butter, plus extra for greasing
- 75g condensed milk
- 175g soft brown sugar
- 100g golden syrup
- pinch ground ginger
- 400g jumbo oats

Preheat the oven to 160°C/gas 3. Line a roasting tin with greased baking parchment.

In a saucepan, melt together the butter, condensed milk, sugar, golden syrup and ginger, then mix in the oats. Pour into the roasting tin, and bake for 30 minutes until deep golden all over.

Remove the tin from the oven and allow to cool before cutting them into squares – I like mine bite-sized to reduce the guilt of eating four.

Goo-goo cake

To sane people, this sweet is too sweet; to those with low spirits (and under-11s), it's just the thing. Those with fillings beware – it is a tooth-yanker.

- 400g condensed milk
- 50g butter
- 100g marshmallows
- 60g Rice Krispies

Line a baking sheet with greaseproof paper. In a non-stick pan, bring the condensed milk, butter and marshmallows gently to the boil, stirring almost constantly to stop it sticking and burning. Cook for 20–30 minutes until it takes on a caramel colour and heavy consistency.

Stir in the Rice Krispies, then spread the mixture over the baking sheet to about 2cm thick and refrigerate to set (about 40 minutes). Cut into cubes to serve.

PICNICS

A grown-up picnic for the opera and other grand occasions (157)
Scotch quail's eggs
Kenyan quiche
Smoked trout and watercress sandwiches
Green beans wrapped in Parma ham
Baby gem and cucumber salad
Strawberries and chocolate

A family picnic (162)
Tortilla
Potato and pasta pesto salad
Cold sausages and pork pies
Cheddar and chutney sandwiches
Chicken and watercress sandwiches
Homemade Jammy Dodgers

Great summer drinks (166)
Vicar's shandy
Dry Pimm's
Old-fashioned lemonade
Iced tea

Here is one of life's few universal truths: food eaten outdoors tastes better. An invitation to a proper picnic is one of the great joys of the summer. Picnics are, after all, a celebration of many things the English in particular are very attached to: good weather, games, gossip, and of course, feasting.

Much of the fun of a picnic – especially if you're going further abroad than your garden – is in the preparation. It's a project that can be the focus of a whole day. It's also tremendously revealing of character: the perfectionist will fuss about the exact spot, number of cushions, sogginess of sandwiches; the hunter-gatherer will arrive full of hope, fishing rod under one arm and berry basket under the other; the games enthusiast will be weighed down with bat, ball, Frisbee, football and kite. Most important of all is to find a spot that is both practical and pretty to set up a base camp; I implore you to make it as far as you can bear from the nearest car.

Although I'm not, in general, a great advocate of kit (mostly because I'm too lazy to carry it) a little goes a long way to making your day comfortable, so it's worth gathering a few key pieces. Mostly it's about priorities – a lunch break on a day's hiking is obviously not about cushions and silver, but there are situations where you'll want to really settle in and enjoy the day in some comfort. Any or all of the following are worth bearing in mind: a blanket (if you're investing, the ones

with waterproofing on one side are great; otherwise, put bin bags underneath), cushions, cutlery, kitchen towel, insect repellent, sun block, corkscrew, frozen wine sleeves, candles or lanterns and matches, torch, portable radio, penknife, rubbish bags. For a grand party, add a real tablecloth and napkins. By the way, a windbreak – however much associated with knotted hankies on heads and lobster-burnt backs – can be the difference between a day of huddling and gritted teeth, and a languorous afternoon with newspapers and napping.

This doesn't mean, however, that it's only with forethought that you can pull off picnicking well. The best one I ever had was perched on the peak of a mountain in the Pyrenees, on a hiking holiday with friends. We were properly hungry, having been walking for several hours with no break, determined to reach the peak before we unwrapped our little parcels. It was a not-quite-summer day, the mountains and valleys that spread out before us from horizon to horizon were the richest of emerald greens, and there wasn't another soul to be seen or heard. Our picnic consisted of nothing but bread, goats' cheese, a handful of nuts and olives, and some dried fruit and chocolate, all washed down by water from a nearby spring.

Great picnic food isn't all about cooking

Never are good ingredients simply prepared as important as on picnics. There's no point in being too precious about the food – if you're having a great day, it will as often as not become seasoned with sand or mud anyway. Buying well is easy and fun but choose one part of the picnic to prepare from scratch and it will all feel much more homemade.

Foods that have their own natural packaging, like hard-boiled eggs and cracked crab claws are ideal as they can be eaten with fingers and create little waste. This is where the ubiquitous sandwich comes into its own; however, anything could – and should – be eaten on a picnic, and the more romantic the better. Just keep in mind how far you have to transport it all – a feast fit for a queen will lose its appeal if you have to drag it up a hill for a couple of hours.

Making a homemade sauce or two for dipping, spreading and to add to sandwiches is the fastest way to lift your bought provisions to a new level, but beware homemade mayonnaise for picnics – it can split easily in heat. Instead, chop any combination of fresh herbs and mix with a good manufactured variety, or bind any combination of fresh herbs with mustard, olive oil and capers to make salsa verde (see page 205) – brilliant for cold meats, fish and potatoes. The Middle Eastern version of mayonnaise is called tahina, and consists of tahini paste beaten together with olive oil, garlic and lemon juice. It is excellent for eating with crudités and pitta. Seek out chutneys that have worked their way to the back of the cupboard and don't forget the ketchup if you've got sausages. I have an embarrassing habit of hoarding mini jams from hotel breakfasts, not for the contents but for the jars, which are perfect for decanting small amounts of mustard and ketchup into. Don't forget to bring some chocolate in whatever form most delights you. Combi-packs of mini chocolate bars go down a treat.

Picnics are the one type of meal that all the guests customarily contribute towards – the Victorians used to draw lots to decide who was in charge of what part of the menu. If you are the instigator of the plan, take your cue from tradition and plan contributions in order to avoid ending up with nothing but hummus and beer. With a very little management, you can end up with a wonderful array of food that appeals to everyone's strengths yet is not taxing in terms of time or money.

Finally, give a thought to presentation. The whole point of a picnic is to get some distance from the trappings of modern life, so eating straight from plastic packaging foils the romance of the plan immediately. Take your provisions home first, get rid of the supermarket packaging and reorganize into tiffin tins, Tupperware, jam jars and flasks, rewrapping whatever necessary in greaseproof paper parcels. You'll be able to protect the contents much better, packing them according to their size and needs, but most importantly, unwrapping each one will be a pleasure.

A GROWN-UP PICNIC FOR THE OPERA
AND OTHER GRAND OCCASIONS
Feeds six

Scotch quail's eggs

I love these tiny versions of the English classic. Allow them to cool thoroughly on kitchen towel before packing, to prevent them going soggy. I like to use Cumberland sausages, as the herbs give a bit of a kick.

- 12 quail's eggs
- 450g best sausagemeat, or sausages squeezed from their skins
- flour, for dusting
- 1 egg, beaten
- 50g 'fresh' breadcrumbs (2 slices stale bread, whizzed into crumbs)
- sunflower oil, for deep-frying
- salt and black pepper

In a small saucepan of water, boil the eggs until hard – about 3 minutes. Drain and run the eggs under the cold tap until they are cool enough to handle. The easiest way to peel them is to first tap one end to break the shell, and peel off the cracked shell to expose a little white. Then slide the handle of a small teaspoon under the shell and use it to carefully work off the rest of the shell.

Divide the sausagemeat into 12 balls (around 50g each) and flatten them into discs. Wrap each around a quail's egg, making sure they are sealed all around. Roll in flour, then in the beaten egg, then in the breadcrumbs, which you have seasoned with a little salt and pepper.

Pour the oil into a saucepan so that it is no more than half-full. Heat the oil until it's sizzling and deep-fry the balls, in batches if necessary, for about 7–8 minutes or until they turn a deep golden toffee colour all over. Leave them to cool on a bit of kitchen towel, which will absorb any grease.

Kenyan quiche

The trick to successful quiche is not to expect it to turn out exactly the same every time: sometimes it will be low and dense, at others light and springy – it probably depends on your mood when you make it. This one is rich and quite strong, far from the flaccid eggy tarts you'll find ready-made.

To explain the name: in truth there's nothing Kenyan about it apart from the fact that Sam found it in a book while on holiday there.

for the pastry
- 225g plain flour
- pinch salt
- pinch mustard powder
- 115g chilled butter, cubed
- 50g Gruyère cheese, grated

for the filling
- 3 tablespoons olive oil
- 2 large onions, sliced
- 1 red bell pepper, deseeded and sliced
- 3 egg yolks
- 350ml double cream
- 1 garlic clove, crushed
- 175g Cheddar cheese, grated
- 2 tablespoons Dijon mustard
- 2 large tomatoes, thickly sliced
- 2 sprigs of basil
- salt and black pepper

To make the pastry, combine the flour, salt and mustard powder in a mixing bowl and rub in the butter until the mixture resembles breadcrumbs. Stir in the grated Gruyère, then just enough water to bring the mixture together in a ball. Wrap in clingfilm and put in the fridge.

Preheat the oven to 200°C/gas 6. To make the filling, heat the olive oil in a frying pan and fry the onions and bell pepper until soft. In a mixing bowl, beat together the egg yolks, cream, garlic, Cheddar and some seasoning.

Roll the pastry out to a circle about 5mm thick and use it to line a 23cm loose-based flan tin. Spread the mustard over the base of the pastry case. Cover with the tomato slices, then add the onion mixture and finally pour in the egg mixture.

Bake for 20–25 minutes, then reduce the oven temperature to 180°C/gas 4 and continue baking for 25 minutes more, or until the quiche looks firm and golden on top. Take it out of the oven and shred the basil over it. Eat warm or cold.

Smoked trout and watercress sandwiches

I find smoked trout a more interesting treat than smoked salmon. To make fresh horseradish cream, see the recipe on page 117.

- 2 fillets smoked wild trout
- 4 tablespoons horseradish cream
- 6 slices soft brown bread

- butter, slightly softened
- 50g watercress
- salt and black pepper

Mash together the trout and horseradish cream, adding a tiny pinch of salt and a scramble of pepper. Butter the bread and spread the trout mixture between the slices, dividing the watercress equally between them. Cut into quarters, crusts off if preferred.

Green beans wrapped in Parma ham

These might seem a bit fiddly, but they're a great way to get some greens into finger food, which can be quite difficult.

- 300g fine beans

- 4 slices Parma ham

Top and tail the beans. Bring a saucepan of salted water to a rolling boil, add the beans, and once they have returned to the boil, cook for 5 minutes. You want them with just a little bite, rather than crunchy. Drain the beans and plunge them immediately into a bowl of cold water. Drain again and allow them to dry.

Rip each slice of Parma ham lengthways in two. Divide the beans into eight piles, so that they are lying together lengthways. Wrap each bundle in a strip of Parma ham and lay snugly into a small airtight container that just fits them all.

Baby gem and cucumber salad

A classic, crunchy salad that can also be eaten with your fingers as long as you chop the lettuces lengthways and leave them attached at the heart.

- 3 baby gem lettuces
- ½ cucumber
- 3 tablespoons good olive oil
- 1 tablespoon sherry vinegar
- salt and black pepper

Quarter the baby gems lengthways. Sliver the cucumber as finely as possible and lay over the lettuce.

Mix together the olive oil and sherry vinegar, then scramble in some salt and pepper. Take the dressing in a separate container to the salad, adding it when you're ready to eat.

Strawberries and chocolate

For pudding, nothing will beat ripe English strawberries along with very dark chocolate, accompanied by a glass of champagne – the challenge is that you really need three hands.

- 2 large punnets ripe strawberries
- 1 large bar best dark chocolate

Open the wrapper and break the chocolate into shards for everyone to help themselves. No need to hull or chop the strawberries; they're easier to eat straight off their stems.

A FAMILY PICNIC
Feeds twelve

Tortilla

There's something extremely rewarding about a perfectly round, golden Spanish omelette, and partly it's the simplicity and economy of it. Although it does use a lot of olive oil, it needn't be extra-virgin, and you can strain it and use it again for cooking afterwards. This is easiest to make in a smallish, non-stick frying pan, about 25cm across.

- 500ml olive oil
- 700g waxy potatoes, peeled and thinly sliced
- 2 large Spanish onions, sliced
- 6 eggs
- salt

Heat all but a couple of tablespoons of the oil in a non-stick frying pan until it moves a little, but is not so hot that it prickles and spits. Add the sliced potatoes and cook for 5 minutes over a medium heat – you want to boil the potatoes in the oil, so that they soften but don't colour. Stir them occasionally to make sure that they do not stick.

Add the onions and a little salt and continue cooking for about 10 more minutes. When the vegetables are soft, strain them in a colander, reserving the oil so that it can be used again for cooking.

Beat the eggs in a large bowl with salt to taste and add them to the potatoes, stirring once.

Heat a tablespoon of the remaining oil in the frying pan and, when it begins to smoke, pour in the egg mixture. Cook for 5 minutes, or until the underside is golden and set, shaking the frying pan gently so that the omelette does not stick, and pushing the edges down evenly.

Invert a dinner plate over the frying pan and turn it all upside down so that the omelette flips onto the plate, gooey side down. Add another tablespoon of oil to the pan, turn the heat up high, and slide the omelette uncooked-side down into the pan.

Reduce the heat to medium and continue cooking for 3 or so minutes before checking whether it's ready. Feel the middle of the omelette – it should be firm.

Slide the omelette onto a clean plate to cool before cutting it into squares or diamond shapes.

Potato and pasta pesto salad

This is a classic Ligurian pasta combination. You will have to adjust the different cooking times according to the size of your potatoes and your choice of pasta.

- 300g tiny new potatoes, halved
- 250g short pasta (I like corkscrews or bow ties)
- 200g fine beans, topped and tailed
- 4 tablespoons fresh pesto (see page 270)
- olive oil (optional)
- salt and black pepper

Bring a large pan of generously salted water to the boil and add the potatoes. Once the water has returned to the boil, cook the potatoes for 5 minutes before adding the pasta. Bring back to the boil, cook on for 5 minutes, then add the beans, and boil everything together for a final 5 minutes.

Drain and allow to cool. Put the pesto in a large bowl, loosening it with a little extra olive oil if you like. Add the pasta and vegetables and toss very thoroughly. Taste and adjust the seasoning as necessary.

Cold sausages and pork pies

Nothing becomes any picnic quite so well as a mound of cold sausages with some mustard and ketchup for dipping. I like to cook up two or three different flavours so that you get a surprise when you go back for more.

As far as pork pies are concerned, I have to admit to being a snob about them. I only like handmade ones that you find in butchers and delis, where the filling is brown rather than a greasy pink, but Ed disagrees vehemently with me, so the choice, of course, is yours.

Cheddar and chutney sandwiches

I'm never sure whether it's more fun to take sandwich ingredients along to a picnic for everyone to mix and match themselves, or to make sandwiches more prosaically in advance. It's probably useful to have a few ready to eat, in case you're shaking with hunger by the time you find your perfect spot and need something to be getting on with.

Cheese sandwiches are as good as anything for this, and I'm not going to give you a recipe. Only to say that grating hard cheese does make it less claggy in a sandwich, and that there are a hundred exciting chutneys out there – they're all great with Cheddar. My current favourite is smoked chilli jam.

If you like tomato in yours (who doesn't, when they are good?) take a few along whole, and slice and add them to the sandwiches at the last minute, so that they don't make the bread soggy.

Chicken and watercress sandwiches

The trick, I find, to great chicken sandwiches is to use good butter rather than mayonnaise, which, if it isn't homemade (and it generally isn't) tends to make them bland. If you find them too dry like this, grab a beer.

- butter, slightly softened
- 12 slices soft white or multi-grain bread
- 3 cooked chicken breasts
- 50g watercress
- salt and black pepper

Butter the bread as you like it, but don't be stingy: it's an ingredient here, not just a sticking agent.

Slice the chicken breasts thinly and pile on half the bread slices, depending on how deeply filled you like your sandwich (I'm very English and mean about fillings, you may prefer a bigger bite, American style).

Scatter with watercress before capping with the rest of the buttered bread. You may like good sea salt inside if your butter isn't salted but you won't need much pepper as the watercress will do the job for you.

Homemade Jammy Dodgers

I defy anyone to resist a homemade Jammy Dodger, and they're great for picnics as the filling won't leak out. Be brave with your choice of jam – rose, if you can find it, is spectacular. This amount will make about 12.

- 120g flour quantity almond pastry (see page 275)
- 8 teaspoons jam

Preheat the oven to 190°C/gas 5. Roll out the pastry so that it's 3–4mm thin. I often find this pastry crumbly and difficult to manipulate, in which case I will cut it into five or six pieces first and then roll each out and cut them up in turn. I'm not fussy about the final shapes of the biscuits – fingers seem to be easier to manage than rounds, but you may have more luck than me.

Sandwich the jam between the cut pastry and bake for about 15 minutes until they turn golden. Allow the biscuits to cool properly on a wire rack before packing carefully.

GREAT SUMMER DRINKS

Vicar's shandy

We learnt to make this drink from friends who live in the roasting hills of Andalucia. It's a much less sickly variation of Pimm's that could probably take cucumber and fruit too, if you like. They drink it in the early evening, when you're ready for a proper drink but it's still too hot to take anything seriously.

- 1 bottle good dry Fino sherry
- 1 litre Sprite
- a fistful of mint sprigs
- plenty of ice

Mix the sherry, Sprite and most of the mint in a large jug. Pour into long glasses filled with ice and a couple of extra mint leaves.

Dry Pimm's

I prefer the No.5 Cup, which is vodka based. If you're feeling wicked, add an extra slug of vodka. Put the fruit and the Pimm's base in a sealable container to macerate, then add the fizzy stuff as you drink it. Err on the weak side to start with, adding more alcohol gradually – too much and it tastes filthy.

- mint, cucumber, strawberries, peaches, sliced lemons and oranges
- 1 part Pimm's
- $1^1/_2$ parts ginger ale
- $1^1/_2$ parts lemonade
- ice

Put the mint, cucumber and fruit in a large jug and pour the Pimm's over it. Leave them to stand for at least 15 minutes before adding the ginger ale and lemonade. Pour into long glasses filled with ice and serve.

Old-fashioned lemonade

This is Constance Spry's recipe, never bettered.

- 3 unwaxed lemons, plus 1–2 extra slices
- 3 tablespoons sugar
- 1.2 litres boiling water
- 1 sprig mint
- ice

Wipe the whole lemons and cut them into dice, being careful not to lose any juice. Put them into a jug with the sugar. Pour in the boiling water and leave to sit for half an hour until strong but not bitter.

Strain the mixture and return the lemonade to the serving jug along with the mint and fresh lemon slices. Keep in a cool place for an hour before serving over plenty of ice.

Iced tea

Iced tea is extremely refreshing and much more pleasant to make yourself than to buy flavoured with something fake. If you'd like a hint of fruit, peach is particularly wonderful: you only need to cut a ripe peach into small pieces and add them to the jug. For picnics, decant the tea, once it's very cold, into a flask.

- black tea leaves
- sugar
- ice
- bunch mint leaves, crushed

Make strong tea in a teapot – an extra spoon of leaves will do the trick. Stir in the sugar to taste and allow it to infuse for 15 minutes.

Strain the tea and leave to cool completely, then pour it into a jug with plenty of ice and the fresh mint; the ice will melt and dilute the tea naturally.

BARBECUES

An informal but manly barbecue (177)
Marinated steak with chimichurri sauce
Guacamole
Cherry tomato salsa
Barbecued pineapple

A Greek-ish barbecue (181)
Butterflied leg of lamb
Greek salad
Tabbouleh
Tzatziki
Upside-down berry tart

An all-American bbq (185)
Sticky ribs
Homemade burgers
Sausages
Potato salad
Tomato and onion salad
Mrs Manson's pink dip coleslaw
Roast garlic bread
Corn on the cob
Triple chocolate chunk cookies

how a man a fire and wave some meat in front of him, and he regresses by a few millennia (in evolutionary terms) before you've managed to mutter 'marinade'. He's also unlikely to let you get between him and the fire until the party's over and it's time to clear up. It's for this reason that many women have never cooked on a barbecue.

The truth is that if you're having a girls-only gathering, you may well be eating outside, but you probably won't bother lighting the barbecue. Before your hackles rise, I'm just being realistic. No matter whether man is actually more accomplished at using fire than woman, the fact remains that he guards this domain wolfishly.

Get over it, or get into it. If, as a woman, you're prepared to get sweat in your eyes and smoke in your hair, learning how to light and cook on a barbecue is extremely satisfying, not to say useful for an easy but delicious spread. But bear in mind that the actual cooking part of the proceedings is also only one side of the ritual of a barbecue; assembling the salads whilst chatting over a beer, or draping yourself over the garden furniture is just as important a role.

Whichever you make your own, give a silent nod to all the smoky gardens across the country filled with the happy chatter of people lounging away a summer afternoon together. There'll only be a few days a year where the company, weather, and geography intersect but when they do, it's a blessed moment.

The basic rules of barbecuing are few but important:

• Barbecue over embers or glowing coals, not flames. The former caramelize the sugars in the meat (this is why gas barbecues work too), while the latter scorch them, resulting in the all-too-familiar sooty crust.

• Trim the meat of nearly all fat, and wipe off oily marinades before cooking – if fat melts down onto the fire, it will burn and infuse whatever you are cooking with acrid smoke, as well as rekindling flames. Instead, brush the food with a very little oil to prevent sticking and drying.

Deciding between gas and charcoal can be difficult. There's no question that the ultimate outdoors cooking experience is over a large, properly built barbecue, filled with a mixture of aromatic woods and coals carefully tended until there's nothing but a heap of glowing embers. Unfortunately, for most of us, this remains an ideal. The small charcoal home barbecue is a sort of halfway house and takes some skill to manage, but if you've got the knack, it can be effective.

And then there's gas: those who've converted to gas swear that there's no difference in flavour. I'm not entirely convinced, and for me, much of the romance is lost in the instant gratification of the blue flame. What is great about a gas barbecue is that you immediately have a very large, all-weather grilling surface enabling you to tackle much bigger pieces than you'd grill using an oven, like butterflied legs of lamb and spatchcocked chickens.

That said, please don't take it all too seriously. While staring into the depths of barbecues gives blokes something to bond over, barbecue bores like any other food snobs deserve to be spit roast very slowly whilst everyone else gets on with enjoying the day.

How to make barbecue food interesting

The general attitude to barbecue food is to buy as much meat as possible and torch it. This is not your only option. Instead, become focused on a good spread of flavours, textures and colours. The main difference from cooking indoors is that you'll be cooking on a large grill, so you've got more space to do something interesting.

It's for this reason that I'm a big fan of choosing a large cut instead of doing a mixed grill – a huge slab of steak to share, a whole rack of ribs – as I think too much variety gets overwhelming and is ultimately unsatisfying.

Variety in the sides, however, does work well, and there are many to choose from, though two or three at any one time will do fine. Look at them in terms of colour: you'll want something green (salad leaves) for sure; red speaks of the summer (tomatoes with either onion or basil and mozzarella) and something comfortingly pale: potato salad is a surefire winner, or failing that a loaf of great bread.

Fish and vegetables are often overlooked on the barbecue, but they can be fantastic. Since many white fish are so delicate they need to be protected from the rasping heat of a barbecue, I prefer to choose more robust, oily ones like sardines, mackerel and mullet. These are traditional fish found on the grill in the Mediterranean and are not endangered by overfishing. Even with these fish, you need to wait as long as you can before cooking – until the fire has really died down – as they can only survive gentle heat.

Dispense with marinades (fish needs to be as fresh as possible) and simply brush them with a little olive oil to prevent sticking. Fish cook very quickly over a barbecue. When they're ready, the skin will blacken and the flesh will become white and flaky. Sardines can take as little as a minute or two on each side; mackerel and mullet will be more like 3–4 minutes. Prawns skewered onto sticks and grilled for a couple of minutes each side are excellent, too – leave the shell on to protect them. Accompany with a little herb oil (page 173), salsa verde (page 205), or chimichurri sauce (page 177).

Vegetables sliced thinly lengthways then brushed with a little oil and seasoned – in particular peppers, courgettes, aubergines and fennel – cook beautifully on the barbecue, but the problem is they take up a tremendous amount of real estate on the grill, becoming a real labour of love for the cook. They are best planned for few, rather than a large party. Skewer them into kebabs to make more room for other food on the grill, but cook fairly slowly and expect them to take longer than you'd like. Alternatively, you can grill them to your heart's content in advance and eat tepid or cold as a salad, dressed in olive oil, crushed garlic and a little lemon juice or sherry vinegar, with plenty of salt and pepper.

Marinades and quick tricks

Marinades are key to distinctive barbecuing. Herbs and spices mixed with oils or yoghurt or blended into nut pastes can be wonderful for enhancing flavour and tenderizing meat, and prevent it from drying out on the grill. Make sure they're oil rather than water-based (apart from yoghurt, which works as a tenderizer) as this will keep them from drying out on the fierce heat.

For flavours to properly steep into meat, you'll need to begin a day or two in advance, but any time spent marinating is better than none. Put the meat into a deep bowl and cover with the marinade, turning a few times. A resealable freezer bag also does the job very well and allows you to massage the marinade in. If you can start the day before, return the food to the fridge, turning every so often, and allow the meat to come back to room temperature for 1–2 hours before you begin to cook. If you only have a few hours or less, leave it covered outside the fridge, which will enable it to steep faster. All but a thin film of oil should be wiped from it in order that it doesn't drip down and cause flames to flare up and scorch it.

For impromptu gatherings, the barbecue cook should have a couple more tricks up his or her sleeve. Herb oils are the easiest way to lift flavours and have the added advantage of keeping for months once you've made them. Mix into olive oil singly or in combination any of the following: rosemary, oregano, marjoram, thyme, tarragon, coriander, parsley, basil and bay. Season with salt and pepper, add a crushed garlic clove and/or the zest of an unwaxed lemon and/or a fresh bird's-eye chilli, and macerate for a few days or as much time as you have before using. They will keep for months if you make sure the oil always fully covers the herbs; make at the beginning of the summer and you'll be sorted for the season (they're also delicious drizzled over bread anytime).

If you haven't had time to marinate, flavoured butters make a great immediate sauce for meat, fish and vegetables. Add to softened butter, at a ratio of about one to three, pounded fresh herbs, spices, anchovy and garlic. Roll the butter into a cylinder in foil and freeze for ten minutes to set. A slice on top of anything just off the grill will pool into a perfect accompaniment, as long as the flavours are complementary.

A trick with rosemary sprigs

Rosemary sprigs make perfect skewers for meat, fish or vegetable kebabs. They look beautiful and suffuse the dish with their distinctive aromatic flavour.

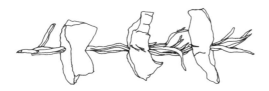

Barbecuing tips for charcoal and wood

It's important to stay away from as many chemicals as possible when lighting a charcoal grill. Don't be tempted to squirt interim fuel over to encourage a slow flame or you'll douse the food with it. Be patient and work on your fire-stoking skills instead.

Cooking over live fires is all about getting the coals or wood glowing at the optimum heat, but with no flames. Here are some strategies for coping with live fires:

- Don't over-pack the barbecue – it will make it too hot.
- Keep a cool spot in your barbecue that has no coal under it. This will allow cooked food to release its fat onto an area that won't throw up flames – it will still be close to the fire so will still cook.
- If it does flare up when cooking, take the meat straight off the fire and allow the flames to burn out. Then close the lid and starve the fire of oxygen (this only works with small flames and barbecues with lids).
- Keep an eye on the food the whole time and move it around from cool to hot spots according to how it's doing.
- Never, ever throw water onto a charcoal barbecue – it may douse the flames but will also throw ash up over the food.

For those who choose the path of gas

Gas barbecues are much faster at heating up, but they're not immediate. It's important to allow the bars of the grill to heat up properly in order that they will sear the exterior of the meat and the sugars will caramelize. Since there aren't flames and embers to go by to test temperature, it's best to do it by feel. Ed uses the 'three-second rule': when a barbecue is at the right temperature, you should be able to hold your hand about six centimetres over it for no longer than three seconds. As a general rule, it's best to heat it up on a medium setting for a good ten to fifteen minutes first – and then once it's properly hot, reduce the setting a little to maintain the heat. The great advantage of gas grills is that you can continue to adjust the heat depending on what you're cooking. *The River Cottage Meat Book* has useful information on the best heat for different cuts of meat, but see the 'Fast Cooking' section for frying and grilling, rather than 'Barbecues', as it has no truck with gas.

Sam and Mark's summer party

This tradition began the year their son Alf was born, when they bought the field they can see from their bedroom window. An old oak tree stands at its heart amidst wild grasses, which grow into a sort of African wilderness as the sun bakes its way through the summer. The party takes place beneath it each year, perhaps a little lovelier each time as the tradition takes root.

The first year, Sam and Mark borrowed a rectangular Indian tent, wrapped in canvas with what must be an Indian return address, written in Hindi. It was white on the outside, a mellow custard inside with red embroidery. I remember the forecast being glorious – two long, hot days that would melt into evenings warm enough to leave the sides of the tent up, but cool enough for shawls and a bonfire. We would feast on a huge wheel of Brie, wrapped in foil and melted on the barbecue, followed by meat grilled to juicy perfection, washed down with a river of red wine. There were kilims and cushions spread around for lounging on afterwards.

Getting everything ready was an undertaking Victorian in magnitude, encouraged by music blaring from the car stereo and a large bucket of iced beer. We all had our jobs and they started first thing: Sam put the meat to marinate, then podded piles of peas, Mark pounded herbs from the garden for pesto and then decided the mint beds were out of control and went on a fierce raid for cocktails. Under Sam's beady eye, I was in charge of the table. It was long and thin, made up of white-tableclothed trestles, with tin jugs of sweet peas, mismatched plates and cutlery, and giant napkins (there was only enough for one for every two people so we had to share, which turned out to be quite bonding). Just as we were finished, Kate arrived looking glamorous, asking what she could do to help.

Somehow, by eight, we were all scrubbed, changed, made up, and very hungry. Immodest of me, I know, but the table looked beautiful. Tea lights that came into their own after dark twinkled from the branches of the tree. Mark pummelled the mint to make big jugs of mojito while Sam and I figured out the seating and wrote names on strips of masking tape which we stuck to the back of each chair.

As the guests arrived, Mark lit the bonfire. In the light of its sparks crackling up into the evening sky, you could see other tents pitched around the field for the children to crash out in later. Small clusters of people were silhouetted against the gloaming, their voices floating across on the slight breeze. You could smell the smoke of the barbecue as the fire began to draw people towards it. One side of the tent was open and the table sparkled welcomingly inside. The great tree stretched out protectively over the whole scene, and I remember very clearly thinking that I would go back again and again to this mental snapshot, as an unfading reminder that summer always returns.

Sam's decorating and lighting tips for eating outdoors

There are differences to arranging an occasion outdoors, in terms of lighting and decoration. Here are some things to think about:

• The wind will be your biggest enemy – think hurricane lamps, glass lanterns over candles. Or put sand into the bottom of large glass vases and wedge candles inside – either fat candles singly, or classic dinner table candles in clusters.

• Tea lights, while much beloved by most, are hard to keep alight outdoors. Old tins, punctured, make good containers, as do jam jars. You can then put them into white paper bags, which will glow gently and protect them from the wind.

• If you have an electricity source outside, fairy lights strung up in the manner of a washing line look great, particularly strings of multi-coloured ones.

• People will gather towards where the lights are, so group them accordingly.

• Make sure there is some kind of light source wherever people might rest food, drinks and ashtrays. Look for unusual places to hang them – branches, walls or windowsills all look romantic.

• Lighting the path between the house and the table is a good idea, and worth doing at the beginning of the evening; dusk always falls faster after several beers.

• Cut sprigs from nearby trees and flowers will be the most harmonious decoration. Either jam into jugs or simply lay across the table.

• The bigger the jumble of plates, bowls and glasses, the more relaxed the occasion will seem.

AN INFORMAL BUT MANLY BARBECUE
Feeds six

Marinated steak with chimichurri sauce

This is real elbows-on-the-table stuff, best eaten with crusty sourdough bread.

- 2kg sirloin steak, in as few large
  pieces as possible

for the marinade
- juice of 1 lemon
- 1 red chilli, finely chopped
- 2 garlic cloves, pounded until smooth
- 1 teaspoon ground cumin
- 1 teaspoon hot smoked paprika
- 100ml olive oil
- sea salt and black pepper

for the sauce
- large bunch flat-leafed parsley, leaves
  picked
- small bunch coriander, leaves picked
- 4 tablespoons sherry vinegar (or red
  wine vinegar)
- 2 tablespoons lemon juice
- 1–2 red chillies, finely chopped
- 1–3 garlic cloves, pounded until
  smooth
- 2 teaspoons ground cumin
- 2 teaspoons hot smoked paprika
- 200ml olive oil
- sea salt and black pepper

Put the meat and the marinade ingredients into a plastic bag and leave for 1–24 hours in the fridge.

To make the sauce, either pulse all the ingredients together in a machine until rough but combined, or pound in a large pestle and mortar (if you are doing the latter, you'll need to chop the herbs first).

Bring the meat back to room temperature and wipe off all but a little of the marinade before cooking. It will need 4–6 minutes on each side.

Set the cooked steaks aside, loosely wrapped in foil on a chopping board, to rest for 10–15 minutes. Pass them around for people to help themselves by carving as much as they want into strips. There should be plenty for a couple of helpings each.

Guacamole

You can either mash this until it has a reasonably smooth consistency, or chop small so that it makes more of a salad. Some people argue for chopped tomatoes to be included, but I prefer mine without.

A trick with avocados that enables you to make this a couple of hours in advance: when you remove the stone, drop it into a glass of water so that it is fully submerged, and leave near the bowl of flesh. Strange but true, it will not go brown.

- 3 large avocados, preferably hass
- 5 tablespoons olive oil
- juice of 1 lemon
- 2 tablespoons Worcestershire sauce
- 1 tablespoon soy sauce
- a shake of Tabasco sauce, to taste
- 1 small red onion, very finely chopped
- 3 tablespoons finely chopped coriander leaves
- sea salt and black pepper

Mash all the ingredients together with a fork and season to taste. A potato masher is good to use if the avocados are ripe but still firm.

Cherry tomato salsa

This has quite a Spanishy feel to it. You could add a finely chopped chilli if you'd like to spike it with some heat, or exchange the parsley for basil and omit the paprika for a more Italian flavour.

- 250g cherry tomatoes
- 1 medium red onion, chopped
- small bunch of flat-leafed parsley leaves picked and chopped
- 2 teaspoons paprika
- 100ml good olive oil
- 4 tablespoons sherry vinegar
- sea salt and black pepper

Pulse together, or chop finely and mix, the cherry tomatoes, red onion, parsley, paprika and some salt and pepper.

Combine the oil and vinegar in a jug and add in a slow stream, mixing or pulsing all the time.

Scrape the salsa into a bowl and allow the flavours to develop for a couple of hours before eating, if you can.

Barbecued pineapple

Cook this fruit after the meat. It will be juicy and sticky and taste vaguely of steak but this only adds to its charms.

- 1 pineapple, peeled and sliced into 1cm rounds
- 75g melted butter
- freshly ground black pepper

Spread the pineapple slices out on a large surface and brush one side with melted butter, scrambling over a little pepper.

When you are ready to eat, grill the pineapple buttered-side down on the barbecue, and brush the rest of the butter on the virgin side. Turn when it begins to blacken and continue grilling until the other side is done.

A GREEK-ISH BARBECUE
Feeds six to eight

Butterflied leg of lamb

The yoghurt's live cultures make this meat incredibly tender over time. You need to prepare it a few days in advance in order for it to really get to work, but a few hours is still worth it. The fun of this is basically to make posh homemade doner kebabs in pitta bread, briefly grilled at the last minute on the barbecue.

- 1 leg of lamb, butterflied – ask your butcher to do this for you
- olive oil
- salt and black pepper

for the marinade
- 500ml plain live yoghurt
- juice of 2 lemons
- 6 garlic cloves, crushed
- 1 tablespoon dried chilli flakes
- 4 tablespoons chopped rosemary
- black pepper

Mix the marinade ingredients together and slather over the meat. Put in a large plastic bag and massage it in. Leave for 3 days in the fridge if you can; if not for as long as you have. Bring the meat to room temperature 1–2 hours before cooking.

Get the barbecue moderately hot. Wipe the marinade off the meat, brush with olive oil and season generously. Cook for about 15 minutes on each side, turning whenever it looks likely to burn. If the fat is dripping down and causing the flames to flare up, put some foil between it and the barbecue until the fat has rendered off. Discard the fat, return the meat directly to the grill and continue as before.

Cut through the thickest part of the meat to see how it's doing – you want it to be quite rare when you remove it, as it will continue to cook as it rests. When you think it's the right side of underdone, remove from the barbecue to a warm place and leave to rest for 15 minutes under some foil.

Carve the lamb into slices and serve with pitta breads or homemade flatbread (see page 271) toasted on the barbecue.

Greek salad

I like the robust chunkiness of a traditional Greek salad. The feta complements the lamb beautifully, particularly if stuffed into a sandwich together.

- 1 cucumber
- 3 large ripe tomatoes, cut into chunks
- 120g black olives
- 1 small red onion, finely sliced
- 1 cos lettuce, cut into ribbons
- small bunch flat-leafed parsley, leaves picked and roughly chopped
- 200g feta cheese, cubed
- 1–2 garlic cloves
- 120ml olive oil
- juice of 1/2 lemon
- 1 teaspoon dried oregano
- salt and black pepper

Peel your cucumber by cutting it in half crossways, and, flat disc side down, run the blade in long horizontal sweeps just under the skin, to remove it in long strips. Chop into fat discs, and then again into half moons.

Combine the cucumber in a bowl with the tomatoes, olives, onion, lettuce, parsley and feta.

Pound the garlic clove(s) with salt until smooth and beat in the olive oil and lemon juice to make a dressing. Pour over the salad, tossing with confidence. Some of the feta will crumble and begin to dissolve, but this is very much to the salad's advantage.

Add plenty of black pepper (the salty feta may preclude the need for extra salt) and sprinkle with the oregano before serving.

Tabbouleh

This fresh herby salad needs to be assembled at the last minute so it doesn't become soggy and disappointing.

- 75g bulghur wheat or cracked wheat
- juice of 2 lemons
- 100ml olive oil
- 250g flat-leafed parsley, leaves picked
- 75g fresh mint, leaves picked
- 175g spring onions, finely sliced
- 3 tomatoes, diced
- salt and black pepper

Boil the bulghur in twice its volume of water for 10 minutes, then drain well. Pour over the lemon juice and olive oil and leave it to sit and absorb the flavours as it cools for half an hour or so.

Finely chop the parsley and mint, removing as much of the stems as possible.

Mix all the ingredients together just before eating, and taste for seasoning. You may like to add extra olive oil or lemon juice, remembering that the salad must taste very sharp and fresh.

Tzatziki

My childhood summers were spent in Corfu, and this wonderfully breathy dip takes me right back.

- 1 large cucumber
- sea salt
- 3 garlic cloves
- 500ml Greek yoghurt
- 2 tablespoons finely chopped mint leaves
- 1 tablespoon olive oil
- black pepper or paprika (optional)

Grate the cucumber into a large sieve or colander and sprinkle with salt. Leave it to drain for half an hour.

Pound the garlic with a little salt to a paste with a pestle and mortar, then add a couple of tablespoons of the yoghurt and blend well. Stir the garlic paste into the rest of the yoghurt.

Pat the cucumber dry and mix into the yoghurt with the rest of the ingredients. Taste for seasoning – I like a little fresh black pepper with almost everything, but you might not. There may be enough salt already, but then again, you might like more to bring out the piquancy. It can be pretty to scatter a pinch of paprika over the top.

Upside-down berry tart

The berry juice should bleed into the pastry here, staining it with the colours of summer. If the pastry is crumbly and difficult to roll out in a single large piece, roll it instead into strips and patchwork it together with your fingers. It will simply look a little more rustic, but no matter. Serve with Greek yoghurt to keep to the theme.

for the tart
- butter
- 4 tablespoons caster sugar
- 1 punnet blackcurrants
- 1 punnet redcurrants
- 1 punnet raspberries

- 120g flour quantity sweet shortcrust or almond pastry (see page 274 and 275)

to serve
- 400g Greek yoghurt

Preheat the oven to 190°C/gas 5. Butter a cake tin or tart case with a fixed base and scatter one tablespoon of the sugar over it. Add the berries and sprinkle over the rest of the sugar.

Roll out the pastry to 5mm thick and drape it over the top, tucking the sides in between the fruit and the tin. Make a couple of slashes in the middle of the pastry to allow the steam to escape, and bake for 35–40 minutes, until the pastry is golden and the juice is bubbling up the sides and through the slashes in the middle.

Remove from the oven and leave to cool for 15 or 20 minutes. Serve straight from the tin, or, if you're feeling brave, place a large plate over the tin and in a smooth movement, invert both together so the pastry arrives first on the plate, and the fruit on top. Place a dollop of Greek yoghurt on the side.

AN ALL-AMERICAN BBQ
Feeds twelve or so

Sticky ribs

If the ribs are very large, get your butcher to halve them across the bone so they are stubbier, and cut into three- or four-rib sections.

- 1kg rack pork ribs

for the marinade
- 2 large garlic cloves, peeled
- 1 teaspoon salt
- 1 tablespoon soft brown sugar
- 1 tablespoon English mustard
- 100g ketchup

- 2 tablespoons pomegranate molasses (or more ketchup, if you can't find it)
- 2 tablespoons vinegar
- juice of $^1/_2$ lemon
- 2 tablespoons Worcestershire sauce
- 3 tablespoons dark soy sauce
- 1 tablespoon runny honey

Pound the garlic with the salt until it forms a paste, and mix well with the rest of the marinade ingredients.

Put the ribs in a roasting tray or ovenproof dish that fits them compactly. Slather over the marinade, turning and coating very thoroughly, and place in the fridge to marinate for at least a few hours.

An hour before you're ready to cook, take the meat out of the fridge and allow it to come back to room temperature. Heat your barbecue to medium-high. Wipe off the excess marinade, carefully reserving it in the dish. Barbecue the ribs for about 12–15 minutes, turning often, until they are deep golden and chewy.

Put the ribs back into the marinade, and sit the whole dish on the barbecue. Add half a cup of water, and bring the whole thing to the boil, turning the ribs from time to time. After a few minutes the sauce should reduce and become sticky. Cut into single ribs and serve immediately.

Homemade burgers

This should make about 10 patties – not everyone may want one – but you could divide the mixture into however many you like, adjusting the cooking time accordingly. If you can't find lovage, replace it with a fresh herb of your choice, or just omit it.

- 1.5kg very lean mince
- 1 medium onion, very finely chopped
- 2 egg yolks
- lug of Worcestershire sauce
- good dash of Tabasco sauce

- 1 teaspoon Dijon mustard
- small handful lovage, chopped
  (or other fresh herb)
- salt and black pepper

Mix all the ingredients together with your hands, then dampen them and shape the mixture into burgers.

It's hard to be exact about cooking times since the size of burgers varies massively, but you could try a couple of minutes on each side for very rare, and 3 minutes each side for rare to medium rare, and have poke in the middle with a sharp knife to check.

Sausages

Sausages are a joy to barbecue as they have enough fat and flavour without needing to be enhanced. To avoid cremating them, grill for about 10 minutes, turning often until they look perfect on the outside, then remove to a plate. Holding them down with a fork, split them lenthways, making sure the skin down one side remains attached, and butterfly them out. Blast the naked centres on the hottest part of the barbecue for half a minute or so – enough to cook them but not long enough for the fat to drip down and cause the flame to flare up.

Potato salad

I like, most often, to dress potatoes with mint-heavy but garlic-light salsa verde mixed in equal parts with Hellman's mayonnaise. It's a real crowd pleaser, familiar enough not to be scary, different enough to be a little surprising. If you're feeling more sophisticated, forget the mayonnaise and dress simply with the salsa verde, adding a little extra olive oil if necessary. In this case, omit the optional garlic; the potatoes should fragrantly accompany the meat rather than chase it off your plate.

- 1kg new potatoes
- 1 portion salsa verde (page 205)
- 150g Hellman's mayonnaise

Boil the potatoes in plenty of salted water until tender, about 20–25 minutes, depending on their size. Make the salsa verde, including some garlic, and mix thoroughly with the mayo.

When the potatoes are tender, drain them and allow to cool a little before tossing them with the sauce.

Tomato and onion salad

If you can find huge, knobby tomatoes, this salad is the best. It's not worth trying to make it any time apart from when they are in season. It's great for stuffing into burgers.

- 6 large beefsteak tomatoes
- 2 pinches caster sugar
- 2 red onions, peeled
- extra-virgin olive oil
- balsamic vinegar
- salt and black pepper

Slice the tomatoes into slices as thick or slim as you like – horizontally across the middle looks prettier on the plate. Lay them, overlapping a little, on a platter. Sprinkle the sugar evenly over them and season very well.

Slice the onions into very fine rounds and spread them evenly over the top of the tomatoes. Drizzle with olive oil and a very little balsamic vinegar and season very well once again.

If you can, allow the salad to stand for an hour. The onions, for me, aren't really for eating as I can't bear the aftertaste, but I like to leave them to sit together with the tomatoes so they have a hint of onion flavour.

Mrs Manson's pink dip coleslaw

This recipe is adapted from the Manson family's barbecue favourite: pink dip. I've added cabbage to turn it into a gunky and addictive coleslaw, but you could omit it and eat with crudités. It's packed with all those processed ingredients you know should be resistible but aren't.

- 200g Philadelphia cream cheese
- 4 tablespoons Hellman's mayonnaise
- 4 tablespoons ketchup
- 1 garlic clove, finely minced
- Tabasco sauce, to taste
- Worcestershire sauce, to taste
- 1 tablespoon white vinegar
- 1 large onion, finely chopped
- 1 white cabbage, shredded

Mash or beat the Philly, mayo, ketchup, garlic, Tabasco, Worcestershire and vinegar to a smooth paste. Combine the onion and cabbage in a salad bowl, add the dressing and toss, toss, toss.

Roast garlic bread

I have found recently, to my horror, that eating raw garlic keeps me awake at night so I've had to diversify. This roast garlic version is a little mellower but it is nonetheless more-ish.

- 1 whole bulb garlic
- olive oil
- 150g butter, softened
- large bunch flat-leafed parsley, leaves picked and chopped
- 2 baguettes

Preheat the oven to 170°C/gas 3. Chop the top off the bulb of garlic to expose the cloves. Drizzle with a little oil and roast in the oven for 1 hour. Remove and allow to cool. Squeeze out the cloves and pound them enthusiastically with the butter and parsley.

Cut diagonal slashes 2cm apart along the bread, not quite cutting through to make slices. You may need to halve the baguettes crossways. Slather the garlic butter into the slashes, spreading on each slice as best you can.

Wrap in foil and bake on the barbecue for 10 minutes, turning halfway through cooking.

Corn on the cob

Although corn cooks well on the barbecue, I like it best boiled and dripping in salty butter. If you prefer the slightly chewy, smoky barbecued version, remove first the hairy husks, brush with oil and season well all over. Cook over a medium heat, turning often. It should take about 10 minutes for the kernels to turn a deep yellow with toffee-coloured chewy bits. Chop each ear into two or three pieces for easier handling while eating, and have plenty of butter and mayonnaise available.

Triple chocolate chunk cookies

This dough will make about 25 cookies. If you don't want to bake it all at once, you can roll it into a fat sausage, wrap it and freeze it for another time. Allow to defrost overnight in the fridge before baking, and serve with vanilla ice cream.

- 250g butter, at room temperature
- 150g light brown sugar
- 75g granulated sugar
- 2 teaspoons vanilla extract
- 2 large eggs, at room temperature
- 275g plain flour
- 75g good cocoa powder
- 1 teaspoon baking powder
- 1 teaspoon salt
- 150g milk chocolate, roughly chopped into small, gravelly chunks
- 150g dark chocolate, roughly chopped into small, gravelly chunks
- 125g salted macadamia nuts

Preheat the oven to 180°C/gas 4. Cream the butter and sugars together until light and fluffy – easiest with the paddle attachment of a free-standing mixer, but possible with elbow grease. Beat in the vanilla and the eggs one at a time, beating to combine in between.

Sift together the flour, cocoa, baking soda and salt, and add to the butter mixture gradually, with the mixer on low speed. The dough should be thick, and heavy work by now. Stop when just combined, then fold in the chocolate and nuts.

Line a baking sheet with parchment paper and drop the dough onto it in soup-spoon sized balls, flattening the dough with dampened hands. Bake for 12–15 minutes – they will seem underdone but you want them chewy, so fear not.

Remove the cookies from the oven and let them cool slightly on the baking sheet, then carefully remove them to a wire rack to cool completely.

ROMANCING AT HOME

Middle Eastern promise (197)
Rack of lamb with rose petal sauce
Persian rice
Baklava
Fresh mint tea

Japanese exotica (203)
Avocado and pink ginger mash
Japanesey tagliata with watercress salad
Frozen berries with hot white chocolate sauce

Refined but not restrained (205)
Baked bream with salsa verde
Claire's elderflower and raspberry jelly

A finger feast (208)
Prawns with garlic, chilli and feta
White chocolate and cardamom custard

Of all my friends, Daisy has the best stories about being wooed with food, or not, as the case may be. There was the ex-lover wanting to impress her with his cooking. He returned from the food market with great fanfare, clutching a brace of pigeon, and a bunch of fresh cranberries (he might as well have been hunting with a bow and arrow). It was a humiliating experience for all, not least the pigeons. Another came to stay from abroad, and wanted to make her dinner. He made steak and pasta – plain steak and plain pasta. He left the next day, his tail between his legs. Then there was the silver-haired funny-man movie star she was set up with. She arrived at his house at the appointed time, a little nervous and excited. He took one look at her, ordered the worst Chinese take-away ever and sat eating it in his tracksuit. She didn't hang around.

But the best story is the love story, the man she met over a business lunch, where they shared a plate of marinated fresh anchovies and talked long into the afternoon, sitting on the banks of the Thames. He called her – a year later. She invited him round for lunch at her house, and marinated fresh anchovies for him. They're still together.

Claire, who has some of the best dinners, is constantly setting people up. There was the dinner where she invited a surgeon and asked him to carve the roast chicken. He brought out his own knives and took an hour over it. There was the one where she got excited about a stall of amazing stinky cheeses in the market and everyone was so overwhelmed by the smell they went home early. But there was also the night of the love tagine – a beef and prune one – where half the guests paired off and went home together.

The triumphs and travails of early romance revolve a great part around eating and drinking. It doesn't have to be dinner, though. The first time I fell in love, it was on a Sunday afternoon in the university holidays. I went over for tea and toast and didn't go home for a week. We lived off bread and tea, dawn trips to the flower market, and air.

Earliest dates on neutral ground mean you can mask yourself with make-up and heels, and the distractions of surrounding noise and other people to watch. But there comes a point where home and food become powerful tools of seduction. It's exciting to be in control of your environment and the proceedings. It can also be nerve-racking. Everything takes on more significance – lamps or candles? Wine or beer? Skirt or jeans? There's nothing more uncomfortable than being busted for trying too hard when you want it all to appear effortless.

Do not be too ambitious about what to cook. You'd be going to a fancy restaurant if food was the focus of the evening, and just because you're a wonderful cook, you don't want to play all your trumps at once. Keep it simple and concentrate on the other treats (like yourself).

Seduction

It's exciting to anticipate an evening's seduction, but be realistic about what you've got time to achieve. Stay on familiar ground: this isn't the best time either to gut and fillet a fish or to try a completely new make-up look. Make something really simple, and something you've done before. If this is mid-week, plan and buy your provisions the day before so you need do nothing but assemble them. Try to relax. You've got the advantage of being on home turf – you can pick the music, set the lighting, arrange the furniture.

If you are going to go the whole hog and eat at the table, don't compromise by pretending it doesn't matter. Lay it properly, and in advance; a table laid for two in a dimmed kitchen is always heart-lurchingly lovely. Be unashamed, and prettify with posies of flowers, tea lights and real napkins. Get out any good cutlery, crockery and glasses you have. You can set up the table in a more romantic spot than the kitchen, like in front of the fire if you have one.

If, however, you'd rather everything was more relaxed, load it all up onto a tray and take it over to the sofa. Make sure you've got some kind of surface to unpack onto. You can always lay up your coffee table and sit on cushions on the floor, or have a picnic right off the rug in front of the fire. I once knew a man who used Japanese take-away as a tool for seduction. He'd arrange it on plates on the carpet and feed it to his date with chopsticks.

In general, go for a balance of characterful comfort and artless style, rather than extreme tidiness. Switch off overhead lights and have enough candles everywhere that you can light all the rooms with them without arranging them too self-consciously (if they're new, burn the wicks down a bit first, because obviously you often live by candlelight).

Some advice for the ladies

Wear less rather than more, and not for provocative reasons – everyone sweats when they're nervous and excited. Consider bare feet for the same reason. Neither do you want to wear anything whose waistband digs in when you sit down (beware tight jeans), or you'll reveal red horizontal welts if you get to removing the item.

Without wanting to come over all Belle du Jour, put grooming at the top of the list, even above food (unless you've met a rare and delightful creature who cares more about food than beauty). Waxing, plucking and bleaching need to happen at least a day in advance, and if your hair tends to be difficult, don't leave it until the last minute. Avoid fake tan, it smells strange, whatever it says on the label. Hide ALL grooming materials. I'm all for honesty, but there's nothing wrong with hanging on to some mystery.

Set-ups

In many ways, this is simply a kitchen supper for your friends, the point of which is to either introduce two people, or to invite someone over that you fancy, but want to be subtle about it for the time being. In America, where they're pragmatic about set-ups, the relevant people will always know and plan accordingly. Here, however, we're more likely to pretend that dating's nothing to do with it.

Don't invite anyone you don't trust with your life or your dignity, or who will make a play for your date – having someone you fancy over is tough enough anyway. Invite instead friends who will make you look good by recounting stories of your winning way with dogs/cars/airline upgrade staff. They will need to be briefed about when would be a good moment to declare themselves exhausted/with other plans and remove themselves from the evening completely. Keep it small – six or less – so it's not too stressful. The food itself won't differ from any other supper, so look at 'Supper Around the Kitchen Table', pages 52–53, for menu ideas, but stick to something you know you do well.

MIDDLE EASTERN PROMISE
Feeds two

Rack of lamb with rose petal sauce

This is the same method as the rack of lamb in 'Supper Around the Kitchen Table', page 80, but with different flavours. It is customary to avoid garlic in such situations, but it would be a shame to share your life with someone who wasn't prepared to take it on. Rose petal jam can be found in Middle Eastern and Turkish delicatessens and shops. If you can't find any, replace it with quince or even redcurrant jelly, mixed with a teaspoon of rosewater. The lamb is particularly good with Persian rice. Salad, with an olive oil and sherry vinegar dressing, would happily work too, though spinach or beans could be even better.

- 1 rack of lamb, French trim

for the marinade
- 2 garlic cloves, crushed
- 2 tablespoons rosewater
- 1 teaspoon ground cumin
- 1 teaspoon ground cinnamon
- 1 teaspoon lemon juice
- 1 tablespoon olive oil
- salt and black pepper

for the rose petal sauce
- 3 tablespoons rose petal jam
- 1 tablespoon very finely chopped mint leaves
- 1 teaspoon white wine vinegar
- 1 tablespoon olive oil
- $1/2$ small garlic clove, crushed (optional)
- salt and black pepper

Mix all the ingredients for the marinade together and slather all over the lamb. Put in a plastic bag and leave to marinate in the fridge for at least an hour, but preferably overnight. Turn occasionally, squishing and swirling the marinade around the meat.

An hour before you want to eat, preheat the oven to 220°C/gas 7. Fifteen minutes later, put the lamb the oven. I find it needs 22 minutes for very rare or 26 for medium rare (I like mine on the nose of 24 minutes). Remove the cooked lamb from the oven and wrap it loosely, but seal securely, in foil. Leave somewhere warm to rest for 15 minutes – it can stay like that for a while, even half an hour if necessary.

Make the rose petal sauce by mashing all the ingredients together, adding the garlic if you like. Carve the cutlets into singles, or pairs if you're feeling butch, and divide between plates. Serve the rose petal sauce in a separate bowl.

Persian rice

Despite the number of ingredients, this rice is incredibly easy to make and will forgivingly sit, covered, for 45 minutes once you've switched off the heat. It goes wonderfully with pretty much anything, and because of its nutty robustness, is excellent for plumping up a vegetarian meal. This amount will actually feed three, and scales up beautifully to feed more people on another occasion.

- vegetable oil
- 50g unsalted butter
- 1 small onion, finely sliced
- 25g blanched almonds, roughly chopped
- 25g pistachios, roughly chopped
- 25g pine nuts, roughly chopped

- $^1/_4$ teaspoon saffron threads
- $^1/_4$ teaspoon ground cinnamon
- seeds of 10 cardamom pods, crushed
- pared zest of 1 unwaxed lemon, cut into fine strips
- 225g basmati rice
- salt and black pepper

Heat 1 tablespoon of vegetable oil and 30g of the butter in a frying pan, and cook the onion gently for about 10–15 minutes, until it is just beginning to caramelize. Meanwhile, toast the nuts in a dry pan, soak the saffron in 2 tablespoons of just-boiled water, and mix the cinnamon and cardamom together. When the onions are ready, pour on the saffron water, add the nuts and lemon strips, then remove from the heat.

Rinse the rice thoroughly. Bring a large saucepan of salted water to the boil, tip in the rice and cook fairly vigorously for 5–6 minutes – the grains should be beginning to soften on the outside but remain firm in the centre. Drain and rinse in cold water. You can do everything up to this point in advance.

Now for the all-important crust: 20 minutes before you want to eat, heat 20ml of vegetable oil and the remaining 20g of butter in a small saucepan. When sizzling, spoon in a layer of rice. Cover with a layer of the nut mixture and some salt and pepper and continue layering the rice and nut mixture evenly until you have used them all.

Make three holes in the rice with a spoon handle, wrap the saucepan lid in a tea towel, folding the ends of the cloth over the top, and cover the pan. Leave over a high heat for 4 minutes to get the steam going, then cook on a low heat for 15 minutes.

Quickly lift the lid to test if the rice is cooked. Once it is ready, spoon out the loose rice onto a serving platter, then upend the pan and dig out as much of the crust as you can to lay on top. Mine never stays in one piece so I just scatter the broken bits over the top.

Baklava

You can buy an array of these syrupy nutty confections from any Middle Eastern deli, restaurant, and often from supermarkets which may stock them as 'Greek pastries', but this recipe from Tom Norrington-Davies is surprisingly easy. Be sure to have everything ready before you deal with the filo pastry, which can dry out and go brittle very quickly. This quantity will fit a 28 x 18cm baking tray – there'll be plenty left for breakfast.

- 150g almonds, roughly ground
- 150g walnuts, pistachio nuts or hazelnuts, roughly ground
- seeds of 6 cardamom pods, crushed
- 150g sugar
- 75g unsalted butter
- 6 sheets filo pastry, defrosted if frozen

for the syrup
- 150g sugar
- 1 tablespoon runny honey
- 2 tablespoons rosewater or 2 tablespoons fruit juice
- 2 tablespoons pistachio nuts, roughly crushed

Preheat the oven to 190°C/gas 5. Combine the nuts, cardamom and sugar in a mixing bowl and set aside. Melt the butter gently in a small saucepan. Cut the pile of filo pastry to fit your baking tray – you do not need to be exact about it –

and place the pastry under a damp cloth to help prevent it drying out while you're working.

Line a baking tray with parchment paper and brush the parchment with some of the melted butter. Carefully lay a sheet of filo pastry over it and brush it with butter. Repeat with another sheet of buttered pastry. Top with half the nut mixture, packing it firmly into the tin.

Cover the nuts with the third sheet of filo, brushing it with more of the melted butter. Repeat with another sheet of buttered pastry and cover it with the last of the nut mixture, pressing it down firmly. Add the last two sheets of pastry, each brushed with butter.

Prick holes all over the baklava with a fork, then, using a sharp knife, cut the baklava into diamonds or squares, right through all the pastry layers. Bake for 20 minutes or until golden brown.

To make the syrup, put the sugar, honey and rosewater (or fruit juice) in a pan with 6 tablespoons of water and heat gently until the sugar has dissolved. Leave to burble gently for about 10 minutes until the syrup has thickened.

Remove the baklava from the oven. Pour the syrup all over it, then sprinkle with the crushed pistachios and allow to cool before eating.

Fresh mint tea

A cup of bright green fresh mint tea seems the best way to celebrate the herb's summery abundance. If you're planting it, the smooth-skinned spearmint variety is the most versatile. Some cubes of Turkish delight to eat alongside go down well.

- large bunch fresh mint
- boiling water

Stuff as many mint sprigs as you can into a teapot. Cover with boiling water and allow to steep for a few minutes. You will be able to refill the pot a few times before needing to change the leaves.

JAPANESE EXOTICA
Feeds two

Avocado and pink ginger mash

This is great as a semi-dip to start with. Eat with toast or pitta. See page 178 for a trick to prevent the avocado going brown once you have peeled it.

* 1 avocado
* 1 tablespoon shredded pickled ginger
* 1 tablespoon olive oil
* 1 tablespoon soy sauce
* squeeze lemon juice
* salt (optional)

Mash all the ingredients together to your preferred consistency, adding a teaspoon of the pickling vinegar from the ginger if you like the flavour. Taste and scrunch in a little salt if necessary.

Japanesey tagliata with watercress salad

This is a very juicy way to cook steak, the bars on the grill really caramelizing the sugar in the mirin. Serve with plenty of white rice to mop up the juice. If you can't find the pickled ginger, use 1 tablespoon of shredded fresh ginger instead.

* 400g rump steak, cut 3cm thick

for the marinade
* 1 tablespoon soy sauce
* 1 tablespoon olive oil
* 2 tablespoons shredded pickled ginger
* 1 teaspoon vinegar from the ginger
* 1 teaspoon wasabi
* 50ml sake, or dry sherry
* 2 garlic cloves, crushed

for the salad
* 1/2 cucumber
* 100g watercress
* 2 tablespoons soy sauce
* 3 tablespoons olive oil
* dash of Japanese rice vinegar
* 2 tablespoons shredded pickled ginger

Combine all the marinade ingredients and pour over the meat. Turn well and leave to marinate – for up to 3 days if you like, but at least a couple of hours.

Preheat the grill to a high heat. Wipe off the marinade and cook the steaks fiercely for 2 minutes on each side. Set them aside somewhere warm to rest for 5–10 minutes.

Meanwhile, to make the salad, peel the cucumber and cut it in half lengthways. Scoop out the seeds by dragging a teaspoon down the middle and slice the cucumber into fine half moons. Put in a bowl with the watercress. Whisk the soy sauce, olive oil, vinegar and ginger together to make the dressing.

Carve the meat into fine slices. Toss the salad well with the dressing and divide between two plates, draping the meat strips over the salad.

Frozen berries with hot white chocolate sauce

This is my approximation of the Ivy's famous pudding. Whilst the berries you get there may be a more beautiful mixture of blue-black, ruby red and pale yellow, this sauce is no snob, and will happily perk up a regular packet of frozen berries from the supermarket. If you're inclined to detail, buy the berries fresh and freeze them on a tray laid out carefully in one layer, with a little space in between each. If you buy a bag of frozen berries, take a few moments to winkle the fruit away from the blocks of coloured ice that gather around them, as it will water down the sauce as it cools.

- 100g good white chocolate, broken up
- 80ml double cream
- 200g mixed frozen berries (not strawberries)

Put the chocolate into a bowl that can sit over a pan of boiling water, or the top half of a double boiler if you have one. In a small saucepan, bring the cream just to the boil, then pour it over the chocolate, stirring so that it melts the chocolate. If the chocolate has not all melted, set the bowl over a pan of boiling water and continue to stir until it has. Set the sauce aside until you're ready to use it.

Gently reheat the sauce, stirring to make sure it is smooth and creamy. Pour it directly over the frozen berries and serve immediately.

REFINED BUT NOT RESTRAINED
Feeds 2

Baked bream with salsa verde

If you like strong, fresh flavours, this piquant salsa is singular in how many foods it complements: white fish, almost all meat (cold is best), potatoes and other veg. Sea and black bream have all the best qualities of the overfished sea bass, without the ecology warning. However, bream is quite a hard fish to find, so call your fishmonger and order it in advance.

Making the salsa is truly an approximate art – if you don't like the shout of raw garlic you'll certainly want to leave it out, in which case I'd strongly recommend some mustard. You can also add a few sprigs of other soft herbs such as basil, coriander and dill, but beware tarragon: only add a very little or it will take over.

The sauce can be whizzed for a smoother consistency, but many prefer a rougher texture, which allows you to feel the different ingredients, in which case, chop. It's unlikely, with the anchovies and capers, that you'll need any salt. You can make the salsa verde the day before, so all you have to do on the day is collect the fish and bung it in the oven. Serve with new potatoes and a green salad.

- 500g whole black or sea bream, cleaned, scaled and gutted
- 1–2 sprigs cherry tomatoes on the vine
- 150ml white wine

for the salsa verde
- large bunch flat-leafed parsley, leaves picked
- small bunch mint, leaves picked

- 2–3 sprigs other soft herbs (optional)
- about 6 anchovy fillets, rinsed, depending on how much you like the taste
- handful capers, drained, or soaked and rinsed if salted
- 1–3 garlic cloves, crushed to paste, or 1 tablespoon Dijon mustard (optional)
- juice of $1/2$ lemon
- 75ml good olive oil, possibly more

Preheat the oven to 190°C/gas 5. Lay the fish in a roasting dish, the tomatoes around it, and pour over the white wine. Bake for 20–25 minutes or until the fish is firm and its eyes are cloudy.

To make the salsa verde, chop all the solid ingredients down until they are the consistency you'd like. Add the lemon juice, then whisk in the olive oil until you have a loose, spoonable (rather than runny) sauce.

When the fish is done, serve immediately with the cherry tomatoes and the sauce in a separate bowl, accompanied by new potatoes and a green salad.

Claire's elderflower and raspberry jelly

This is perfect in the summer, and beautiful served in a big glass bowl with cream or ice cream, but needs to be made in advance so it can set. The making part is quick and easy and could be done the night before or easily in 15 minutes before work on the morning of serving.

- 8 sheets leaf gelatine
- 350ml elderflower cordial
- 2 punnets raspberries

to serve
- cream or ice cream

Put the kettle on to boil. Soak the gelatine in cold water for a few minutes, then drain. Pour 100ml of boiling water over the gelatine and stir to fully dissolve.

Allow to cool for a couple of minutes, then stir in the elderflower cordial and 250ml of cold water. Empty the raspberries into a glass bowl (or jelly mould, for more of a flourish) and pour over the liquid.

Cover and put in fridge to set for at least 4 hours – it works best if left overnight. When the jelly just begins to set, give it a good stir, if you remember, so that the berries are suspended in the jelly rather than floating on the top. To remove from the mould, if using, dip the bottom briefly into a bowl of hot water, cover with a slightly larger plate and with one confident movement, invert the mould so that the jelly lands neatly onto the plate. Serve the jelly with the cream or ice cream.

A FINGER FEAST
Feeds two

Prawns with garlic, chilli and feta

This recipe belongs to Tessa Kiros, but it is such a treat for an easy, light but utterly tasty supper for two (or as a starter for four) that I couldn't resist including it. I love it not just for the flavour, but for the sticky finger-licking process of peeling the prawns and sucking up the sauce with the shells, which is undeniably sexy.

While the combination of shellfish and feta sounds unlikely, the cheese melts into the sauce, becoming more of a seasoning than an ingredient. It tastes to me of the long hot nights ringing with the sound of cicadas during the childhood summers we spent on Corfu.

It couldn't be quicker or simpler, layering the ingredients in the pot all ready to go bar the actual cooking, which only takes a few minutes. If you are concerned about the sustainability and ethics of eating prawns, seek out cold-water varieties. Serve with a soft green salad and crusty white bread, or rice, to mop up the juices.

- 1kg large uncooked North Atlantic prawns, shells and heads on (frozen and defrosted is fine)
- 100g butter
- 4 garlic cloves, finely chopped
- handful flat-leafed parsley, chopped
- 2 red chillies, deseeded and finely sliced (or a few drops Tabasco)
- 200g feta cheese, roughly crumbled
- juice of 2 lemons
- salt

Rinse the prawns thoroughly. Dot one-third of the butter over the base of a casserole, then spread a layer of prawns over it and season with salt. Sprinkle with one-third each of the garlic, parsley and chilli (or a few drops of Tabasco). Layer away until the ingredients are finished and put the lid on.

When you're ready to cook, turn the heat to medium-high and cook for 5 or so minutes, shaking from time to time, until the prawns have more or less turned pink. Scatter over the feta and add the lemon juice. Reduce the heat and cook for another 5 minutes, grasping the dish firmly and continuing to shake determinedly from time to time.

When the prawns are coral-coloured throughout, transfer the whole pot directly to the middle of the table along with a small ladle, so you can help each other to plenty of sauce.

White chocolate and cardamom custard

You can either churn this into ice cream, or serve as a cold custard, which is wonderful with soft fruit, particularly poached pears. It's fine to make 24 hours in advance and will keep in a sealed container in the fridge or freezer.

To transform into ice cream, churn in an ice cream-maker for 30 minutes and then freeze, or put it straight in the freezer, remembering to break up and stir in the crystals every half an hour until the mixture is properly frozen. You will want to soften it for a few minutes at room temperature before serving.

- 150ml full-fat milk
- 50g white chocolate, grated
- seeds of 5 cardamom pods, pounded
- 2 medium egg yolks
- 50g caster sugar

- 150ml whipping or double cream

to serve
- soft fruit or poached pears

Combine the milk, grated chocolate and cardamom in a saucepan and heat gently, stirring from time to time, until the milk steams and tiny bubbles prickle at the side of the pan. Remove from the heat and set aside to cool a little.

Whisk the egg yolks and sugar together in a bowl. Slowly stir in the hot milk mixture. Rinse out and dry the milk pan and return the custard to it. Then – and this is the difficult bit – cook over a medium-low heat, stirring, until the mixture thickens enough to coat the back of a spoon, being careful not to let it overcook and curdle.

Remove the custard immediately to a cold bowl, stir in the cream and allow it to cool fully, stirring occasionally. Serve with soft fruit or poached pears.

AFTERNOON TEA

A very traditional tea (216)
Cucumber sandwiches
Scones with clotted cream and jam
Lemon drizzle cake

A warm winter tea (219)
Toast with anchovy butter and boiled eggs
Buttered crumpets dripping with honey
Rich and muddy chocolate brownies

A celebratory girly tea (221)
Potted crab with best brown bread
Mixed berries and cream
Magnolia Bakery cupcakes

A high tea with kids (224)
Soft-boiled eggs and Marmite soldiers
Banana sandwiches
Homemade fresh fruit yoghurt
Daisy's no-cook chocolate biscuit cake

A wheat-free tea (226)
Rye or pumpernickel toast with mashed avocado
Almond and orange-flower cake

A hot chocolate drink, and a cold one (229)
Extra-rich hot chocolate
Chocolate milk

ea is an easy sell; there's no downside. As well as being appealingly old-fashioned, it's cheap, fun, and baking is a great way to fill a rainy afternoon with kids (does anyone grow out of licking the bowl?) There's no greater innocent pleasure than that found in slivers of cucumber packed into crustless, buttered white bread, so fresh it sinks to almost nothing between your teeth, or a piping-hot pot of china tea, so delicately scented that it infuses the whole room with a feeling of well-being. Coming in from a rain-swept walk with friends, face blasted by wind, to a doorstep of white toast, salty butter pooling on its surface, followed by a sticky orange or lemon drizzle cake and a big slug of hot tea is an experience worthy of export.

Yet at home when I was growing up, tea was never much cop. It was always a healthfully disappointing part of the day – more of an ellipsis than a meal – involving brown toast and Marmite, and juice, with the occasional Madeira cake at the weekend. Sometimes Kate would pull off a banana sandwich with strawberry milk, but that was as exciting as it got. My idea of a real afternoon tea comes from childhood weekends with my oldest friend Min. There was always an eye-popping spread involving white toast laden with melting butter and golden syrup, Wagon Wheels, Jammy Dodgers, and chocolate milk to dissolve each sticky, thrilling mouthful.

Afternoon tea can be either the most grand or informal of occasions. Whether you choose to get out your matching china or settle down with a big mug, tradition requests the hostess to pour out the tea for her guests. They can then help themselves to any food that is laid out, resting their plates on side tables, to be enjoyed preferably near a roaring fire, or in the summer, under a shady tree.

Varieties of tea leaf

There are four main types of tea that we drink – beyond that there are several thousand varieties and blends. The leaves in their truest form are:

• Black tea: what we most commonly think of as tea, it is fully fermented and roasted for the characteristic dark colour and high levels of caffeine.

• Green tea: made from leaves picked young, it has a light flavour and is packed with antioxidants.

- Oolong tea: rare and fine, with a smoky, amber liquid and a floral, fruity quality.
- White tea: the rarest type, it is unfermented and simply dried. It has a subtle, mellow flavour and very pale colour.

The different afternoon teas and their characters

Afternoon tea is generally black tea, and ranges widely in depth and flavour. Indian is strong, deep and often bitter, and takes milk well, while Chinese is light and fragrant, and traditionally drunk without milk:

- Assam: a strong and malty Indian brew. Good as a breakfast tea.
- English Breakfast: a robust blend, unscented and popularly drunk at any time.
- Darjeeling: a light, unscented Indian tea.
- Earl Grey: a delicate tea, fragranced with Bergamot. A popular tea-time tea.
- Lapsang Souchong: smoky scent and flavour, traditionally drunk weak.

The perfect cup of tea

In idler moments, I have tested many different ways of making tea, from the most basic bag-in-a-cup to the fanciest loose leaf in various pots. For the perfect afternoon cup:

When the kettle has boiled, pour a little water into your pot and swirl it round for a minute to warm it throughout. Discard the water. Add two heaped teaspoons of Earl Grey or Lapsang Souchong (depending on your mood) and 1 heaped teaspoon of Indian (I stick to English breakfast) leaf tea and cover with the boiling water. Stir briefly, put the lid on and allow it to steep for 2–3 minutes before pouring.

When setting the scene

Relinquish yourself utterly to unreconstructed femininity. Decide what surface in your sitting room will make the best tea table and cover it with a cloth or, even better, the old flowered bedspread at the bottom of the cupboard. Buy or pick a posy of pale, scented flowers to jam into a jug. Group chairs and sofa together for optimum chatting. Bring your toaster and toastables in from the kitchen (you may need to clear another surface for them). Remember to remove the packaging before you bring the food through – it's ugly and noisy, and a constant reminder that you're not living in 1840, which of course, whilst taking tea at least, you'd really much rather be. Stack the eating plates on the same table as the food, as well as some napkins and forks, and let everyone help themselves while you pour out the tea.

It is not important to have a tea-set. Lucky you, of course, if you inherited your grandmother's old set from the fifties – dig it out and spare a kind thought for those of us lesser mortals making do with mugs. Yes, tea does taste better from china fine enough for the light to shine through, but it doesn't make it a happier meal, so in the end, it doesn't matter. If your teapot is less than pretty, make a kerchief out of a dishcloth or napkin to wrap around the pot, tying the ends through the handle to secure it. It will function doubly to keep the pot hot and to camouflage it. If you have a matching tea-towel you can lay it out under the pot, and the repeating pattern will smarten up other mismatches you might not like.

A VERY TRADITIONAL TEA
Feeds six

Cucumber sandwiches

I like the finest scraping of Marmite in mine, instead of salt and pepper.

- unsalted butter, slightly softened
- 12 slices very soft white bread
- ¹/₂ cucumber, peeled
- salt and black pepper

Butter the bread and season with salt and pepper. Cut the cucumber into paper-thin slices and divide evenly between the bread. Trim off the crusts and cut each sandwich into four long fingers. Eat before they go soggy.

Scones with clotted cream and jam

Serve scones warm from the oven with strawberry jam and clotted cream.

- 225g self-raising flour, plus extra for dusting
- 60g butter, cubed
- pinch salt
- 30g sugar
- 150ml milk
- 1 egg, beaten (optional)

Preheat the oven to 220°C/gas 7. Put the flour, butter and salt in a large bowl and rub lightly with your fingertips until it forms dusty breadcrumbs – you can achieve this with a few pulses in a whizzer, too. Add the sugar, then the milk in quarters, squelching or pulsing until you have a sticky but thoroughly blended dough.

Turn out onto a well-floured surface and knead for a couple of minutes. Roll out the dough until 2.5cm thick, then cut into 6 to 8 rounds with a cookie cutter or the rim of a glass. Dust a baking sheet with flour and put the scones on it. Brush the tops of the scones with beaten egg if you want a shiny finish, or dust them with flour. Bake for 15 minutes, or until golden and risen.

Lemon drizzle cake

This is a truly easy version you can mix all at once if you have a whizzer. If not, follow the traditional cake method by creaming the butter and sugar first , then beating in the eggs, and finally the flour and milk. It will feed more than four, so there'll be plenty left over for breakfast the next day – keep it wrapped up in an airtight container.

for the cake
- 150g butter
- 150g caster sugar
- 150g self-raising flour
- 3 eggs
- finely grated zest and juice of 2 large or 3 small unwaxed lemons

- 2–3 tablespoons milk

for the drizzle
- juice of 2–3 lemons
- 120g granulated sugar

Preheat the oven to 180°C/gas 4. Line a loaf tin with greaseproof paper. Beat all the cake ingredients together with an electric whisk or in a blender until you have a smooth batter. Pour the mixture into the tin and level the surface. Place the tin on the middle shelf of the oven and bake for 50–60 minutes, or until a skewer inserted in the centre comes out clean.

Remove the cake from the oven, prick it all over with a fork and allow to cool for 1 minute. Combine the lemon juice and granulated sugar and, stirring all the while, pour and spoon it carefully over the cake. Leave in the tin until it has thoroughly cooled.

A WARM WINTER TEA
Feeds six

Toast with anchovy butter and boiled eggs

Anchovy butter was fashionable in the twenties and thirties. Its saltiness perfectly sets off a soft-boiled egg, but it's good spread thickly on toast anytime. You'll find it's also fantastic for perking up grilled steak or lamb – just cut a thin slab straight onto the meat when it's done and allow to melt as you eat. It will keep in the fridge for a couple of weeks.

- 40g unsalted butter
- 8 anchovies, drained of oil and patted dry
- 6 slices thickish white bread (I like sourdough almost always)

to serve
- 6 soft-boiled eggs

Pound the butter with the anchovies until thoroughly combined.

Lightly toast the bread and allow it to cool for a minute on a rack so as not to get soggy. Spread with the paste and serve with the soft-boiled eggs.

Buttered crumpets dripping with honey

The world is divided between people who like jam on crumpets, and people who prefer something both sweet and dripping. Although I find it hard to countenance, there are those who like to eat them with a savoury topping, but in every case it is extremely important to drench them in butter whilst they are piping hot, so that they are soggy and juicy on the inside, and still a bit crispy on the outside.

So toast the crumpets, at least two each, and butter them before piling on to the plate. Serve the honey (or jam, or golden syrup – and Marmite or cheese if needs be) separately for everyone to spoon over the crumpets.

Rich and muddy chocolate brownies

Brownies are one of my favourite things. You could omit the nuts and cherries if you like, or replace with other fruit and nuts, but for goodness' sake not with glacé cherries.

- 400g best dark chocolate, with 70 per cent cocoa solids
- 300g butter
- 4 eggs
- 300g sugar
- 1 teaspoon vanilla extract
- 50g flour

- 50 finely ground almonds
- $^1/_2$ teaspoon baking powder
- pinch salt
- 100g whole macadamia nuts (salted, strangely, are best)
- 150g ripe cherries or dried cherries, stones removed

Preheat the oven to 180°C/gas 4. Line a baking tin with foil and parchment.

Melt 300g of the chocolate with the butter in a heavy-based saucepan over a very low heat. Chop the rest of the chocolate roughly and set aside. When the chocolate mixture has melted, set it aside to cool a little.

In a mixing bowl, beat together the eggs, sugar and vanilla until pale and creamy. Add the melted chocolate mixture and beat well.

Sift together the flour, almonds, baking powder and salt, and fold into the brownie mixture with a metal spoon. Stir in chopped chocolate, macadamia nuts and the cherries, being careful not to knock out any of the air.

Scrape the batter into the prepared baking tin and bake for 30 minutes. The top will have risen and cracked a little to reveal the dark gunge within. To test, prod with a fork – the tines will come out sticky but without raw mixture on them. If it seems too soft, return to the oven for 3 minutes but remember that it will continue to cook as it cools, and that an overcooked brownie is a thing of beauty spoiled forever.

A CELEBRATORY GIRLY TEA
Feeds six

Potted crab with best brown bread

The method here is the same as for potted shrimp and makes a refreshing change. Once made, cover and refrigerate – as long as the crab is completely covered by its butter cap, it will keep happily for several days, if not weeks.

- 150g butter
- 3 pinches ground mace
- 2 pinches cayenne pepper
- a little freshly grated nutmeg
- 200g mixed brown and white crabmeat
- salt

Melt the butter gently with the spices. Switch off the heat, add the crabmeat and allow it all just to sit together quietly for about 10 minutes, so the flavours can get to know each other.

Taste for salt and divide the mixture between ramekins, coffee cups or whatever you want to serve it from. Store in the fridge until the day of serving but take the chill off it before eating (with bread or toast) so that the flavours can come into their own.

Mixed berries and cream

As obvious as it may sound, nothing becomes a summer celebration quite so much as a mound of naked berries – whichever kind look the best at the time – accompanied by a tub of best double cream. Wash it down with a bottle of icy champagne. Think classic rather than cliché.

Magnolia Bakery cupcakes

The Magnolia Bakery in New York was made famous by a *Sex and the City* scene where the girls met there for cupcakes. And deservedly so – it's full of beautiful people who look like the cast of *SATC*, except younger, and the cupcakes are amazingly delicious, sickeningly sweet, and pretty as you like. This is their recipe for sponge – it can be used for cupcakes (which, to keep in the spirit, should be iced in pastel-coloured butter icing – plenty of it) or for a basic sponge cake. If you don't fancy the icing, which in reality is more pleasing to look at than to eat, I find, just sift some icing sugar over the top instead. This recipe will make 24 cupcakes.

- 175g unsalted butter
- 350g caster sugar
- 4 large eggs
- 200g self-raising flour, sifted
- 150g plain flour
- 250ml full-fat milk
- 1 teaspoon vanilla extract

for the icing

- 400g unsalted butter, softened
- 250g icing sugar
- food colouring, in whatever colours you fancy

Preheat the oven to 180°C/gas 4. Prepare two cupcake tins by filling each hole with paper cups.

Beat the butter in a freestanding mixer or with a hand mixer until smooth, gradually adding the sugar until it becomes pale and creamy. Continue to beat for a further 3 minutes or so until fluffy.

Add the eggs one at a time, beating well to combine between each. Sift the flours together and, with a metal spoon, fold into the mixture a quarter at a time, alternating with the milk and vanilla. Be careful at this point not to over-beat and release the air.

Spoon the batter into the cupcake papers, filling them to just over halfway. Bake for 20 minutes or until golden on top – they're ready when a skewer inserted in the middle comes out clean. Remove them from the oven and leave to cool on a wire rack.

To make the icing, beat together the butter and icing sugar, adding a few drops of the food colouring of your choice. This is the only time I like my pastels Dulux-pale. When the cupcakes are cool, slather the icing generously over the top.

A HIGH TEA WITH KIDS
Feeds four

Soft-boiled eggs and Marmite soldiers

Boil the required number of eggs for 4–5 minutes. Serve with toast spread with butter and Marmite and cut into soldiers.

Banana sandwiches

Kate's childhood special. The bread must be very fresh.

- 6 slices brown bread
- butter, slightly softened
- 2 bananas
- 1 tablespoon runny honey

Lightly butter the bread. Mash the bananas with the honey and spread over half the bread, topping the sandwiches with the remaining slices. Trim off the crusts and cut the sandwiches into triangles.

Homemade fresh fruit yoghurt

I like to use fruit sugar (fructose), which is available from all health food stores and supermarkets, instead of sugar when cooking for kids, as it has a much gentler sugar release, and is less likely to send them on sugar rushes.

- 400g soft fruit, such as peaches, raspberries, blueberries, or plums
- 30g fruit sugar
- 450g wholemilk organic yoghurt

Peel the fruit and cut into chunks if necessary. Put it in a small saucepan along with the fruit sugar and a little water. Cover and gently simmer until soft, about 10 minutes. Allow the fruit to cool. Push the cooled fruit through a sieve to remove seeds or pips, then stir it into the yoghurt.

Daisy's no-cook chocolate biscuit cake

Kids love making this because you get to bash biscuits in a plastic bag with a rolling pin, and the whole process is very quick, which means they don't get bored. Daisy gave me this recipe which is always a hit with her nephews. Freeze the leftovers – there should be plenty – it's equally delicious to snack on straight from the freezer.

- 1 x 250g packet digestive biscuits
- 125g dried sour cherries (or cranberries)
- 125g dried apricots, cut up into chunks
- 200g dried sultanas or raisins

- 150g butter
- 3 tablespoons golden syrup
- 1 tablespoon black treacle
- 200g dark chocolate, broken (or milk chocolate, or a combination, for kids)
- icing sugar, for dusting

Line a 23cm-square low-sided baking tin with baking parchment.

Empty the biscuits into a large plastic bag, seal it, and whack, pummel and crush with a rolling pin until they are reduced to a sandy rubble – the finer the crumbles, the less likely you are to come across great wedges of boring biscuit in the finished product. You can also do this in a food processor.

Put all the dried fruit in a bowl and add the crushed biscuits. Melt the butter, golden syrup, black treacle and chocolate together in a bain-marie until smooth. Pour into the biscuit and fruit mixture and stir well.

Empty into the baking tin, making sure not to scrape it out too thoroughly and spoil the licking part. Smooth over the surface and leave in the fridge for at least 2 hours. To serve, dust with icing sugar and cut into fingers with a sharp knife.

A WHEAT-FREE TEA
Feeds four

Rye or pumpernickel toast with mashed avocado

There's a little café in downtown Manhattan called Gitane where I always used to meet my friend Eve for tea and this was my favourite thing to eat there.

- 2 avocados
- 4 tablespoons olive oil
- good squeeze lemon juice
- Worcestershire sauce, to taste
- 4 slices rye or pumpernickel bread
- salt and black pepper

Mash the avocado with the olive oil, lemon and Worcestershire sauce, adding salt and pepper to taste.

Toast the bread (pumpernickel will need double toasting to get rid of its natural dampness) and spread thickly with the avocado mixture.

Almond and orange-flower cake

Kate, who has convinced me that white flour is the very devil, inspired me to make this cake. It is dense and damp and very straightforward to produce, if you have a whizzer. If you don't, buy the almonds ready-ground and roll up your sleeves for some heavy work. Serve with fresh berries, if you like.

- 225g butter, cubed, plus extra for greasing
- 75g polenta flour, plus extra for dusting
- 225g blanched almonds
- 225g caster sugar
- 1 teaspoon baking powder
- 3 eggs
- finely grated zest of 1 unwaxed orange, and juice of $^1/_2$ orange
- finely grated zest and juice of $^1/_2$ unwaxed lemon
- 2 tablespoons orange-flower water
- icing sugar, for dusting

I like a loaf tin here, don't know why, something to do with my childhood, but a 21cm springform tin will be the right size, too. Butter it, then shake some polenta flour all around the inside and tip off any that doesn't stick.

Preheat the oven to 170°C/gas 3. Toast the almonds in a dry pan over a fierce heat for a few minutes, stirring often, until they begin to colour very lightly. Transfer to a food processor and whiz until fine.

Add the butter, sugar, polenta flour and baking powder and whiz again until you have a fine mix that is beginning to ball up like very heavy marzipan. Add the eggs one at a time, pulsing until absorbed, then add the citrus zest and juice and orange-flower water. Give it one good final blast to check the mixture has combined evenly, then pour the batter into the prepared tin.

Bake for 50–55 minutes, until the top is golden all over and a skewer inserted in the middle comes out clean. Wrap in tin foil and leave to smugly sit and improve for a day if you have the time, or just allow to cool and dust with icing sugar before serving.

A HOT CHOCOLATE DRINK AND A COLD ONE
For four

Extra-rich hot chocolate

I prefer this with longlife milk as it has a rich creaminess that works well when sweetened, and I have to admit being partial to the canned spray cream here, too. So shoot me.

- 4 tablespoons unsweetened cocoa, plus extra for dusting
- 1 litre full-fat milk
- sugar, to taste (or fructose)
- glug of rum (optional)
- whipped cream

Boil a little water in the kettle. Divide the cocoa between four mugs and pour over a tablespoon each of boiling water, stirring until fully dissolved.

Heat the milk gently, until just on the point of boiling, and divide it between the mugs, stirring as you pour it in. Taste and add a little sugar (or fructose) if you like – you may well not. Now is the time to add your glug of rum if you want it.

Balance a spoonful of whipped cream on each to finish and dust with cocoa.

Chocolate milk

You can turn this into a delicious mocha by adding a shot of espresso to it.

- 4–6 tablespoons unsweetened cocoa
- 2–3 tablespoons sugar (or fructose)
- 1 litre full-fat milk
- ice

Boil a little water in the kettle. Put the cocoa and sugar into a jug and add a few tablespoons of boiling water (or freshly made espresso if you are making mocha). Stir until smooth. Gradually add the cold milk, stirring all the while. Serve in long glasses over ice.

WEEKENDING WITH FRIENDS

A Saturday lunch in summer (239)
Granny's gazpacho
Fennel tarte tatin with goats' cheese and thyme
Pancetta, cherry tomato and butter bean salad
Soft lettuce, avocado and fresh pea salad
Marinated mozzarella
Chocolate raspberry meringue sandwich

A Saturday supper for vegetarians (243)
Mushroom, leek, walnut and Roquefort pie
Poached plums with yoghurt and shortbread

A Sunday lunch in deepest winter (246)
Slow-roast lamb with melting vegetables
Rhubarb crumble

A Middle Eastern wintry Sunday roast (248)
Pomegranate roast chicken
Butternut, aubergine and chickpea stew
Saffron mash
Orange-flower treacle tart

A supper for making in advance (253)
Great fish pie
Tarte tatin

Food that kids love (256)
Sugar-roast ham
Homemade pizza
Spaghetti with Lina's mini meatballs
Crispy duck with pancakes

Soup for unexpected visitors (261)
Pea and blasted garlic soup
Cucumber and yoghurt soup

Drinks for the weekend (262)
Elderflower cordial
Bloody Mary
Bullshot

The perfect weekend balances between peaceful lolling and pointed activity. It should not involve too packed a schedule – if you're moving too fast you'll miss those moments of silent unity that can only really happen whilst idling. Just sleeping under the same roof as friends has a whole different feel to spending a day with them. You catch up by breathing the same air, cooking and eating together. This sort of time is, to me, the closest you can get to those lost student years hanging out in other people's digs, drinking Diet Coke, painting toenails and catching up on who snogged who in the college bar the night before. What might at first seem like aimless chat will often shape itself into rewarding conversation. Beware, however, a weekend without any focus at all – it can seem long, boring and you'll end up eating and drinking yourselves into a cross-eyed stupor.

My favourite weekends away are with Sam and Mark, and not just because they're family. They live in a pretty thatched cottage an hour and a half from London, surrounded by nothing but woods, trees and working farms. By the time I come over the brow of the last hill and turn right down the track towards the house, I can feel the grind of the city melting away. The weekends are reliably familiar, yet never exactly the same. We sleep a lot, walk when the weather is kind, cook and talk, but there's no pressure to do anything. Normally Sam plans a big lunch on Sunday with local friends: a current obsession (season permitting) is slow-roast lamb with the next-door farmer's purple sprouting broccoli, onion dauphinoise and heaps of salad. We have always made easy cooking companions, sharing our stories of the week over the huge walnut chopping board.

My weekends are unashamedly greedy. I could quite happily graze non-stop, and in fact I quite often do. Although I have suggested these menus as lunch or supper, they can all work anytime. I only cook one proper meal of the day; the other can be bread and cheese with the wintry addition of hot soup when the season calls for it. I prefer to invite extras for lunch at the weekend as I like its loungey mobility and it's much easier for people with kids to come over then.

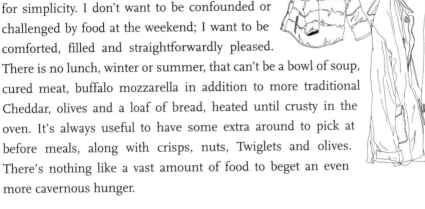

There's something about weekends that calls for simplicity. I don't want to be confounded or challenged by food at the weekend; I want to be comforted, filled and straightforwardly pleased. There is no lunch, winter or summer, that can't be a bowl of soup, cured meat, buffalo mozzarella in addition to more traditional Cheddar, olives and a loaf of bread, heated until crusty in the oven. It's always useful to have some extra around to pick at before meals, along with crisps, nuts, Twiglets and olives. There's nothing like a vast amount of food to beget an even more cavernous hunger.

Having children to stay

Kids can be a great bonus on weekends, encouraging the most sullen of adults to jump in puddles and roll down hills, but bear in mind that they will change the balance and energy of it. Meals need to be more regulated, inclusive activities planned (not endless long walks), and appropriate kit available (you try settling down with the papers when your nephew is colouring in your sofa).

Check with your friend whether there's anything the child won't eat, and then pick something that you can put aside a more simplified version of for the children, tarting it up for yourselves if you want to. Kids tend not to like 'bits', particularly green ones, in their food. Some good general bets are: sausages, mince, pasta, baked potatoes, grated cheese, fruit yoghurts. Don't worry too much about providing a perfect nutritional balance: it's not your problem and one meal won't hurt – parents will most likely just be grateful that someone else is doing the feeding. Keep all the food separate (e.g. pasta and sauce) until you serve it and then you won't have to start again when a small nose gets turned up. For fun, set up a special kids' table for them.

As far as drinks are concerned, it's safer to assume that most parents don't approve of sugary drinks for kids unless it's a special occasion. Getting in some extra milk (and chocolate powder for treats), small cartons of juice, some low-sugar cordial, and a bottle of wine whatever the time of day means you'll please everybody. Ice cream, the cheap stuff, is the best pudding always, or possibly something else with chocolate in it. Sounds like chocolate ice cream to me.

Very small children don't need much to entertain them. Cardboard boxes, crayons, plastic cups, paper plates and feathers can be just as absorbing as regular toys. Plastic bags and anything they can strangle each other with, like ribbon or string, aren't a good plan, but a makeshift dressing-up box with old clothes of yours and cast-off make-up is a winner. Old clothes become dressing-up kit, cranky bits of make-up, face paint.

Kid-proof your home by removing anything obviously valuable, fragile, sharp or edible-seeming. It may look less chic but you won't spend the whole time anxiously watching your friends anxiously watching their kids. Make it clear where they can play and which rooms are off-limits. It's a good idea to turn a corner of the room into their base camp and tell them you've made it especially for them. The more elaborate – with upturned furniture, shawls/towels/throws and cushions involved – the more likely they are to spend time in it.

Give into their schedule and build your fun around it. Otherwise your time will only be spoiled by an irascible child who has missed his or her morning nap. Spend as much time as you can outside. You won't get as stressed by the mess, and the kids will have more space. If you've got room and it's summer, there's little that can match a barbecue and a cheap paddling pool. Otherwise a walk in the nearest park with a children's playground is fine.

Remember how boring it was being dragged around to a random grown-up's house when you were nine and try and be sympathetic to older kids. Talking about your favourite subject at school is a drag; watching a DVD is a bit more fun.

A weekend in the country

In the country, the season will almost always dictate the plan, and the weather will be unrelenting in the part it takes in your decision-making. You'll know who will want to brave the elements and who'd be happier tucked in next to the fire with a stack of DVDs and the papers. If the weekend is not planned around a specific activity, any of the following are possibilities:

• A picnic.

• A proper walk: preferably to a pub – map it and make it a good couple of hours – if you've got two cars, and don't want to retrace your steps, drive both to your destination and leave one there, squashing yourselves into the other to get you to your starting point. If you're having a picnic, leave it in the boot of car one to make your goal even more appealing.

• A local event: find out if there are any country fairs, funfairs, circuses, festivals, or even car boot sales so you've got somewhere to go and poke around.

• A visit: to a nearby pile, castle or gardens.

• Shopping: whether to a particular market, or just to poke around local shops – even a trip to the local charity shop can become a bizarrely exciting outing.

• The sea: traditional seafronts are endlessly fascinating to those who don't live near the sea.

• Games: this is dependent on having all very keen players present otherwise someone will feel excluded and get bored and cross.

• Any seasonal celebration: like an outing to scavenge for blackberries, a fireworks night bonfire, or a midsummer's day picnic.

• A lunch party: make a drizzly winter day all about lunch, and invite a few extras along.

• The papers: which will see anyone through a rainy afternoon.

A weekend in the city

I love it when people come to stay. I get really excited about it, painting my nails and trying on outfits to wear out on Saturday night. Kate often comes to stay – she lives right across town, so the rhythms of her neighbourhood are different from mine. We try to make an effort to go somewhere we haven't been before – a random exhibition, or an expedition to a junk shop or market – though as often as not, we'll end up gossiping in the local nail bar.

Because city homes are generally smaller than country ones, weekends in the city tend to focus on outings. They don't have to be complicated or difficult to organize – the same old errands take on a shiny new patina when you move location. Use it as an excuse to do something you wouldn't normally:

• Shopping: whether for food, clothes, or around a local market.

• High culture: an obscure movie, a play, a concert, an exhibition – if you can't get into anywhere, visiting an unusual museum that's more tucked away will be more original.

• Low culture: bowling, darts, some kind of cabaret/comedy night/football match/ice skating/pool.

• Lunch in a new or favourite restaurant: it always feels more louche than dinner.

• A pedicure: there are few women who'd refuse an unexpected treat like this.

Getting your home ready

It's rare to have the luxury of spending two whole days with friends, so make everything a treat. Use it as an excuse to buy a pretty new bar of soap or an extra bunch of flowers. Give some thought to whether you need to re-arrange any furniture to accommodate extra people.

If your weekend is going to be about chatting with friends, revamp your sitting room by hiding the telly. Or, do the opposite, and plan a huge movie session, setting the room up like the comfiest cinema imaginable, with the toaster and kettle at arm's reach.

A spare room is a special place. Because it belongs to no one, it has a different character to any other room in a home, and can be transformed into a proper haven with a little thought. If you've never slept in it, spend a night there. It's the only way to know whether the radiator works, the mattress is lumpy or the sun streams in at dawn.

• Make sure there is somewhere to hang things up, even if it is just a couple of hangers on a hook on the back of the door.

• If you have an extra dressing gown, hang it there. Your friend may not use it but it'll give the room a dash of luxury.

• Put a posy of flowers or even just a single bloom in a glass next to the bed.

• A bedside lamp within turning-off reach is possibly the most important thing, along with some tissues, a jug or bottle of water and a pair of new earplugs. The sound of country silence can, strange as it seems, be as deafening to townies as the yawning jaws of the 4am rubbish truck to a country-dweller.

• Alien beds can increase insomnia, so make sure there are a few books, old comics and magazines to read.

If you don't have a spare room and the living room is going to double up, you have to be slightly more organized about it:

• Figure out a corner of the room and a surface for clothes as well as some kind of hanging arrangement.

• A sofa can be made to feel just as special as a bed by making it up with proper sheets and pillows.

• Make sure there's a low table and a lamp within reach next to it.

• Tell your friend what sort of time you're likely to be padding around in the morning, or where to find essentials such as tea, if there's a chance that you might sleep in late.

A SATURDAY LUNCH IN SUMMER
Feeds four

Granny's gazpacho

Since my grandmother loathes salad, she has always made gazpacho. She replaces the traditional garlic with onion, but you could revert, using instead a couple of finely chopped cloves of garlic (new season, wet garlic has the freshest flavour). If you have excellent, full-flavoured tomatoes, you will probably not want to use the tomato juice, but if they are slightly failing, replace a couple of them with juice, as suggested below.

- 800g very ripe beefsteak tomatoes, peeled, cored and deseeded, and cut into chunks
- 2 green peppers, deseeded and white pith removed
- 1 small onion, finely chopped
- 1 cucumber, peeled, deseeded and cut into chunks
- 200ml olive oil, plus extra for serving
- 1 teaspoon sugar
- 200ml pressed tomato juice (optional)
- salt and black pepper

In a whizzer, blend the vegetables, oil, sugar and seasoning together first until fairly smooth. Then add the tomato juice, if you are using it.

Push the mixture through a fine sieve, discarding the leftover pulp rather than forcing it through. Chill and serve with an extra glug of olive oil.

Fennel tarte tatin with goats' cheese and thyme

This is a savoury version of the French classic, and is incredibly light but very tasty. You will need a large sauté pan and a small 20cm frying pan with an oven-proof handle for this recipe. Tarte tatin pans are larger so if you are using one of those you will need to adjust volumes accordingly, with another 1–2 fennel bulbs and 100g of pastry to make it fit.

- 3 large heads fennel
- 25g butter
- 4 tablespoons olive oil
- 1 tablespoon fennel seeds
- 4 sprigs thyme, leaves picked from one
- 1 tablespoon Pernod (optional)
- 300g ready-made shortcrust pastry
- 150g goats' cheese log, crumbled, rind discarded
- sea salt

Cut the tops off the fennel, reserving and chopping finely any feathery fronds. Shave a fine layer off the tough bottom, too. Cut the fennel lengthways into quarters, then eighths – they should be like flattish triangles.

In a large sauté pan, melt the butter and add the olive oil. When the butter is beginning to foam, add the fennel seeds and fry for 1 minute. Add the fennel pieces on their sides in one layer, tucking three of the thyme sprigs around them. Scrunch over a generous pinch of salt. Cook gently for 12–15 minutes or until the fennel pieces are just turning golden on one side. Turn them over and repeat, adding the Pernod towards the end if you are using it. When the fennel pieces are soft and golden, remove them from the sauté pan and drain off any excess oily liquid. This can be done in advance.

When you are ready to cook, preheat the oven to 190°C/gas 5, and roll the pastry into a circle about 23cm diameter, or slightly larger than your frying pan.

Pack the fennel into the frying pan as tightly and neatly as possible, aiming to finish with a reasonably flat surface. Drape over the pastry, tucking the excess down between the fennel and pan. Make a single long slash through the middle of the pastry to allow steam to escape and bake for 25 minutes or until the pastry is golden.

Chop the leaves of the remaining sprig of thyme and combine with the chopped fennel fronds. Remove the tart from the oven, place a serving dish over the frying pan and invert the whole thing, allowing the tart to drop onto the plate pastry-side down. Sprinkle generously with the goats' cheese, which will melt into the gaps, and finish with the chopped herbs. Serve warm or at room temperature.

Pancetta, cherry tomato and butter bean salad

The idea of this salad is to be versatile. You could use any spiced or smoked porky bits, like cold or cooked chorizo, parma ham, or leave them out for a fully vegetarian menu. You could also replace the basil with flat-leafed parsley or rocket, and the butter beans with flageolet, or chickpeas, or even pasta, and eat tepid.

- 250g cherry tomatoes, halved
- 1 x 400g tin butter beans, drained
- small handful basil leaves, roughly chopped
- 100g pancetta, cubed

for the dressing
- 2 tablespoons olive oil
- 1 tablespoon sherry vinegar
- 1 garlic clove, pounded to a paste with salt
- salt and black pepper

Combine the cherry tomatoes, butter beans and basil in a bowl. Whisk all the dressing ingredients together and toss them thoroughly with the tomatoes and beans. Season to taste.

At the last minute, fry the pancetta until golden all over and toss with all its tasty fats into the salad.

Soft lettuce, avocado and fresh pea salad

To prevent the avocados going brown once you have peeled them, see the trick on page 178.

- 1 round lettuce, torn
- 1 large or 2 small avocados, peeled and sliced
- 200g ready-shelled fresh peas

for the dressing
- 75ml olive oil
- juice of $1/2$ lemon
- 1 tablespoon Dijon mustard
- 1 sprig mint, leaves picked and finely chopped
- salt and black pepper

Combine the lettuce, avocado and peas in a salad bowl. Whisk together all the ingredients for the dressing and toss very well with the salad just before eating.

Marinated mozzarella

This mozzarella will be even more delicate than usual, so handle it gently.

- 4 balls buffalo mozzarella
- 100ml best olive oil

- small bunch basil
- black pepper

Drain the mozzarella of water and put into a bowl. Add the olive oil and a few turns of pepper and allow the cheese to marinate in the fridge for a few hours.

Remove the bowl from the fridge half an hour before eating and tear the basil leaves over the top.

Chocolate raspberry meringue sandwich

This is actually a recipe for roulade, but I always find it's much easier simply to fold the meringue over once than attempt to roll.

- 4 egg whites
- 225g caster sugar
- 225ml double cream

- 2 punnets raspberries
- icing sugar

Preheat the oven to 180°C/gas 4 and line a baking sheet with baking parchment. In a very clean, grease-free bowl, whisk the egg whites until they stand in stiff peaks. Add the sugar as slowly as you can bear to – a tablespoon at a time is ideal but I'm never that patient – whisking confidently in between.

When all the sugar is absorbed the meringue should be very stiff and glossy. Immediately turn it out onto the baking sheet and smooth into a square 2–3cm thick. Bake for 15 minutes, keeping an eye on it to check it doesn't colour too much.

Remove the meringue from the oven – the outside should be crisp and the inside spongy-wet. Allow to cool for a couple of minutes, then place a board over the meringue, invert it quickly, and peel off the baking paper. Leave it to cool fully.

Whisk the cream until stiff and spread it over the meringue – a spatula is useful here. Scatter the raspberries over half of the square, then flip the other half on top – or, if you're feeling professional, roll it up. Dust with icing sugar to finish.

A SATURDAY SUPPER FOR VEGETARIANS
Feeds four

Mushroom, leek, walnut and Roquefort pie

This is completely vegetarian but so robust that I defy any carnivore to miss the meat. The ingredients here will fit a pie dish about 22cm in diameter and 4cm or so deep.

- 375g ready-made puff pastry
- 300ml milk
- 2 onions
- 2 bay leaves
- few whole peppercorns
- freshly grated nutmeg
- 350g mixed mushrooms, the wilder the better
- 2 tablespoons olive oil

- 60g butter
- 2 leeks, white parts only, cut into 5mm discs
- 1 tablespoon flour
- 100g Roquefort, crumbled
- 50g walnut halves
- small bunch flat-leafed parsley, leaves picked and chopped
- 1 egg, beaten

Divide the pastry into two balls, one twice the size of the other. Wrap in clingfilm and allow to rest for 1 hour.

Preheat the oven to 180°C/gas 4. Put the milk in a saucepan with one of the onions cut in half, the bay leaves, peppercorns and a hint of nutmeg. Bring to a murmur and keep on a very low heat.

Meanwhile, fry the mushrooms in the olive oil until they release all their juices. Set aside, reserving the liquid separately in a jug.

Chop the other onion. Melt half the butter in the frying pan and cook the onion until soft and translucent. Add the leeks and continue cooking over a fairly low heat for 5–10 minutes, stirring from time to time to prevent sticking.

Strain the infused milk into the jug containing the mushroom liquid. In a small saucepan, melt the rest of the butter, add the flour and cook very gently for

2–3 minutes until golden and sandy. Gradually add the milk mixture, stirring constantly so that the sauce is smooth and has the consistency of thick double cream (don't worry if that seems quite thick; it will get thinner and more soupy as the mushrooms release more liquid into the pie).

Bring the sauce to a simmer and cook for a few minutes, still stirring. Remove the pan from the heat and add the mushrooms, onions and leeks, Roquefort, walnuts and parsley.

Roll out the two balls of pastry into circles, lining your pie dish with the larger one and allowing the excess pastry to flop out over the edges. Pour in the filling, then brush some water around the rim of the pie to dampen it. Cover with the other pastry disc, trimming the extra pastry from the edges, and sealing the rim with the tines of a fork.

Fashion the pastry trimmings into whatever you fancy – a couple of leaves, or letters to spell a word – and stick them on with a little water. Brush the whole surface with beaten egg and bake for 40–45 minutes or until the pastry is golden and cooked.

Poached plums with yoghurt and shortbread

If you have some in your garden or window box, you can replace the mint with sweet geranium leaves, which impart a wonderful fragrance to the syrup, as I was taught by the fabulous Irish cookery teacher Rory O'Connell. The recipe will work equally well with apricots, pears and other soft fruit, although you may need to adjust the quantities depending on their size. Serve, if you like, with biscuits – the shortbread on page 141 would be good.

- 175g white sugar
- 4 sprigs mint
- 8 ripe plums

to serve
- 400g Greek yoghurt
- 8 tablespoons runny honey, preferably lavender
- shortbread (optional)

Put the sugar, mint and 350ml of water into a saucepan just large enough to take the plums in one layer. Bring to the boil slowly, stirring until the sugar dissolves. Add the plums (don't worry if they're not completely covered by the liquid), cover, and bring gently back to the boil. Reduce the heat to a just-prickling simmer, cover, and cook for 5–15 minutes, depending on the ripeness of the plums – the more ripe, the less time you will need. The skins will split a little but no matter.

Prod the plums with the tip of a knife and if they seem giving, switch off the heat and allow to return to room temperature slowly – they will continue to cook as they cool. Once cooled, remove, along with the syrup, to a bowl you can serve from (glass is pretty). Place in the fridge if you're not serving them soon, but allow to return to room temperature before eating.

To serve, put the yoghurt in a separate bowl, spoon the honey over it and leave on the table with a plate of biscuits for everyone to help themselves.

A SUNDAY LUNCH IN DEEPEST WINTER
Feeds six

Slow-roast lamb with melting vegetables

I find that shoulder of lamb is the best cut for slow cooking. You could roast it for even longer at a slightly lower temperature, if preferred, and include whatever vegetables will hold their shape, such as fennel or parsnips. Serve with dark minerally greens, lightly steamed to contrast with the melting vegetables.

- 1 lamb shoulder, trimmed of all but a small covering of fat
- 3 tablespoons olive oil
- 10 large garlic cloves, peeled
- 3 onions, quartered
- 2 carrots, halved across and again along
- 3 celery sticks, cut across into quarters
- 4 decent-sized potatoes, thickly sliced
- 2 large tomatoes, quartered
- small bunch thyme sprigs
- 1 bottle white wine
- salt and black pepper

Preheat the oven to 220°C/gas 7. Season the lamb generously and put into a large, deep casserole. Leaving the top off for the time being, put the lamb in the oven to roast for 20 minutes, while you're preparing the veg.

Take the casserole out of the oven, and the lamb out of the casserole. Switch the oven to 150°C/gas 2. Heat some oil in the casserole, add the vegetables and thyme and fry on the stove for a few minutes, turning so that all the vegetables are covered with oil.

Return the lamb to the dish and pour over nearly the whole bottle of wine (it should half-fill the pan, leaving some lamb and vegetables sticking out the top). Season again and bring the liquid just to the boil.

Put the lid on, return the whole dish to the oven and leave to bubble away for 4 or so hours. You can afford to be a bit approximate here, but check every so often if you are there to do so; if for some reason the liquid overflows because your lid doesn't fit properly, top it up with a little water.

When you are ready to eat, carefully lift the lamb out of the dish – it may fall apart, so put it into a bowl or deep serving dish. Dig out the vegetables with a slotted spoon and lay them around the lamb. Drain the excess oil from the remaining liquid and decant it to use as gravy. You will more divide the meat into chunks than carve it, as it will simply fall off the bone. Serve with steamed broccoli – purple sprouting, if in season, seems to go down the best.

Rhubarb crumble

If you don't like ginger, replace it with the grated zest of half an unwaxed orange.

- 1kg rhubarb
- 2.5cm fresh ginger, peeled and grated
- juice of $^1/_2$ orange
- 3 tablespoons demerara sugar

- 90g chilled butter, diced
- 90g sugar – demerara, white, muscovado, or a mixture

for the topping
- 120g plain flour

to serve
- cream or custard

Preheat the oven to 190°C/gas 5. Trim the rhubarb and cut into 2.5cm pieces. Toss with the ginger, orange juice and sugar (taste to check it's enough – rhubarb can be very tart) and spread into a large-ish gratin dish.

To make the topping, put the flour, butter and sugar into a mixing bowl and rub lightly between thumb and fingertips until the mixture resembles breadcrumbs or oats. Scatter the topping over the rhubarb and bake for 35–40 minutes, until the crumble is golden and the fruit is bubbling up around the edges.

Serve with thick Jersey cream, or custard if you prefer (I don't).

A MIDDLE EASTERN WINTRY SUNDAY ROAST
Feeds four to six

Pomegranate roast chicken

Pomegranate molasses makes the skin of the chicken tangy and chewy. If you can't find it, you could just rub some olive oil on the skin and dust with double the volume of spices. Serve this with the chickpea stew and saffron mash shown on pages 250 and 251.

- 1 red onion, halved
- 4 tablespoons pomegranate molasses
- 1 teaspoon ground ginger
- $^1/_2$ teaspoon ground cumin
- 1 clove garlic, pounded to a paste
- 1 lemon, halved
- 1 medium-large free-range chicken

Preheat the oven to 220°C/gas 7. Finely chop one half of the onion, leaving the other half intact. Mix the pomegranate molasses, chopped onion, ginger, cumin, garlic and a squeeze of lemon together in a small bowl and set aside. Stuff the intact onion half in the cavity of the chicken, along with both lemon halves.

When the oven is hot, roast the chicken for 15 minutes, then remove it from oven and slather the pomegranate mixture over the skin. Reduce the oven temperature to 180°C/gas 4, and continue roasting the chicken for 45 minutes. The skin will look black and charred but fear not, it will be deliciously tangy and chewy. If the bird is particularly large, it may need an extra 10–15 minutes' cooking.

Remove the bird from the oven, loosely cover with foil and let it rest for 10–15 minutes before carving.

Butternut, aubergine and chickpea stew

This is a sort of wintry ratatouille, but even better I think. You can roast the butternut at the same time as the chicken. This amount will feed six people as a side dish, or four vegetarians as a main course. It is also delicious eaten cold the next day.

- 1 small butternut squash
- good olive oil
- ¹/₂ teaspoon saffron strands
- 1 onion, finely chopped
- 2 garlic cloves, finely chopped
- 1 x 400g tin plum tomatoes
- 1 teaspoon ground cumin
- 150ml white wine
- 1 large aubergine
- 1 x 400g tin chickpeas
- 3 tablespoons chopped flat-leafed parsley leaves
- sea salt and black pepper

Preheat the oven to 180°C/gas 4. Top and tail the butternut squash and chop it into 3cm cubes, discarding all the seeds. Toss in a roasting tin with enough olive oil to coat all the pieces, and a good scrunch of sea salt. Roast for 1 hour, turning and basting every 15 minutes.

Pour a couple of tablespoons of boiling water over the saffron and allow it to infuse. Meanwhile, fry the onion over a medium heat in a couple of tablespoons of olive oil. When it is soft, add the garlic, turn the heat down and stew gently until the onions are sweet and golden.

Drain the tomatoes, chop them roughly and add to the onions, along with a teaspoon of salt, the cumin, wine and saffron water. Bubble off the alcohol for a couple of minutes over a high heat, then turn the heat down and simmer gently for 35 minutes.

Top and tail the aubergine and cut it into 3cm cubes. Heat 4 tablespoons of olive oil in a separate large sauté pan or saucepan. When it is hot, add the aubergine and fry on all sides until golden and tender – this will take about 15 minutes.

When the butternut is done, remove it from the oven and set aside until just cool enough to handle. While it is cooling, drain the chickpeas of water, add them to the tomato sauce and allow to warm through.

Peel the skin off the butternut, and combine all the ingredients in one of the pans. Serve sprinkled with a little olive oil, salt, pepper and the parsley.

Saffron mash

The key to light-as-air mash is to add the milk when it is at boiling point, and to sneak in an egg white or two. If the mash looks quite gloopy, it can sit, covered, in a low oven for half an hour, and will take on a perfect consistency.

- 500g good, floury potatoes
- 75ml milk
- $^1/_2$ teaspoon saffron strands
- 1 egg white
- 30g butter
- sea salt

Peel and halve the potatoes. Put them in a saucepan of water, bring to the boil and simmer until tender. Drain the potatoes and break them up with a masher.

In a small saucepan, bring the milk and saffron to the brink of boiling and pour immediately into the potatoes, beating with an electric whisk. Add the egg white, whisking all the while, then add the butter.

Salt to taste, but avoid pepper as it interferes with the delicate saffron flavour. Continue to beat until the deep yellow colour spreads throughout the potato.

Orange-flower treacle tart

I like the faint scent you get with the addition of orange-flower water. If pastry stresses you out, grate it evenly over the flan case, pressing it down and up the sides until you have a thin crust all over. It will remain uneven (which adds to its rustic charm) but it's much easier than rolling. This amount will fill a 20cm tin.

for the pastry
- 3 tablespoons orange-flower water
- 120g plain flour
- 60g chilled butter, cubed, plus extra for greasing
- zest of $^1/_2$ unwaxed orange
- pinch salt

- 25g butter
- 250g golden syrup
- 1 tablespoon orange-flower water
- 2 tablespoons orange juice
- finely grated zest of $^1/_4$ unwaxed orange
- 3 tablespoons double cream (optional)

for the filling
- 3 slices day-old white bread

to serve
- thick cream

To make the pastry, put the orange-flower water into the freezer for 10 minutes to get really cold. Meanwhile, rub the flour, butter, orange zest and salt together – or pulse in a whizzer – until the mixture has a breadcrumb consistency. Add the cold orange-flower water tablespoon by tablespoon until the pastry just comes together – you may not need it all. Roll into a ball, wrap in clingfilm and let rest in the fridge for an hour.

Preheat the oven to 200°C/gas 6 and butter the flan case (easy release helps). When the pastry has rested, roll it out into a circle 5mm thick (or grate it as described above) and press into the tin. Return the pastry to the fridge while you make the topping.

Cut off and discard the crusts of the bread and whiz the remainder into breadcrumbs – you should have about 75g.

Melt the butter over a medium heat for a few minutes until it stops sizzling and colours a little – don't have the heat too high or it will burn. This is called beurre noisette, and it has a slightly nutty scent. Set aside for a few moments.

In a separate saucepan, melt all the golden syrup for a few minutes until it softens, then stir in the beurre noisette, orange-flower water, orange juice and zest, and the cream (if using). Add the breadcrumbs and warm through gently for 5 minutes.

Spoon the filling evenly into the pastry case. Bake for 15 minutes, then turn down the oven temperature to 180°C/gas 4 and continue baking for another 20 minutes. Serve the tart straight out of the oven, with thick cream.

A SUPPER FOR MAKING IN ADVANCE
Feeds six

Great fish pie

You can use whatever fish you like here. I like to use mainly pollack, adding squid, scallops and a few North Atlantic prawns for flavour, but some smoked fish (traditionally haddock) will add a good flavour too.

* 1kg mixed fish
* 800ml full-fat milk
* 1 bay leaf
* about 6 black peppercorns
* medium bunch parsley, leaves picked and chopped, stalks reserved
* 100g butter
* 50g plain flour
* 75ml single cream

* 1 heaped tablespoon dill, finely chopped
* 3 heaped tablespoons cornichons, drained and roughly chopped
* 2 tablespoons capers, rinsed and drained
* juice of $1/2$ lemon
* 1.2kg floury potatoes
* 1 egg white (optional)
* salt and black pepper

Preheat the oven to 200°C/gas 6. Put the fish (apart from any squid or scallops) into a large shallow dish – the one you intend to make the pie in is fine. Cover with the milk, and add the bay leaf, peppercorns and the stalks of the parsley. Bake in the oven for 10 minutes, to lightly poach the fish.

Remove the fish from the oven and drain off the milk, reserving it for later. Pick out any bones you can see, along with the bay leaf and peppercorns, and break up the fish roughly. Cover and set aside.

In a large saucepan, melt 75g of the butter and add the flour, stirring over a low heat for several minutes until it turns golden and sandy. Gradually add most of the fishy milk, stirring all the while so that it becomes a smooth sauce – keep back 50–100ml of the milk to use for the mash. When the sauce is thick enough to coat the back of a wooden spoon, stir in the single cream and continue to cook for a few more minutes.

Remove the pan from the heat and stir in the chopped parsley, dill, cornichons, capers and lemon juice, then be brave with the salt and pepper. Pour the sauce over the cooked fish and mix well. It should be quite saucy and runny but will thicken up on further baking. Allow it to cool a bit before scattering over any scallops, squid or prawns you are using.

To make the topping, peel, halve and boil the potatoes in a large pan of water for 25–30 minutes, or until tender. Drain well, return the cooked potatoes to the pan and crush roughly with a potato masher.

Bring the remaining milk back to the boil and add the last of the butter, a good quantity of salt and pepper, and the egg white if you are including one. Mash very well (or beat with an electric whisk), until it is as smooth and fluffy as possible. Set aside to cool.

Spread the mash over the fish mixture. Scrape ridges along the surface with the tines of a fork, and season again. At this point you can leave it in the fridge for a day, or freeze it to use in the future. When you're ready to cook, preheat the oven as described and bake for 45 minutes, until the top is turning golden and the sides are bubbling up. Eat with a mountain of peas.

Tarte tatin

I'm happy to use regular shortcrust instead of rich sweet pastry (both recipes on page 274) for puddings – I like the contrast with the sweet topping, and when you've added cream it's rich enough. Here, you can caramelize the apples in advance and drape the pastry over them and do the final baking when you're ready to eat. Or you can make it in advance and eat it cold. You will need a very clean, heavy-based sauté pan, about 24cm across, with an ovenproof handle, or a tarte tatin pan.

- 150g flour quantity rich sweet shortcrust pastry (or 250g ready-made shortcrust pastry)*
- 120g soft butter
- 150g caster sugar

- 2kg similar-sized cooking apples

to serve
- cream or crème fraîche

Using your fingertips spread the butter over the surface of the pan and up the sides, then sprinkle over the sugar as evenly as possible. Peel the apples, cut in half from top to bottom and remove the core. Some will split, but don't worry too much as you'll want some smaller chunks to pack the pan properly. Standing them upright, with the stalk sides uppermost, pack them as tightly as possible into the pan so that they have no room to move.

Place the pan over a high heat and cook the apples until the butter and sugar begin to caramelize and the apples start to soften, about 10–15 minutes. You need to find the right temperature to caramelize and soften the apples without burning them, so turn down the heat a little if they seem intent on burning, and increase it if there appears to be a lack of colour to the apples and the juice is threatening to flow over the sides. From time to time turn an apple half towards the centre of the pan to check the amount of colour on the base. Once the majority of the apples are a medium gold, the tart is ready for the oven. At this point you can allow them to cool; the last stage will take 25 minutes.

Preheat the oven to 200°C/gas 6. Roll out the pastry to approximately 3cm wider than the diameter of the pan and leave in a cool place. When ready to bake, cover the apples with the pastry, tucking the excess between the fruit and the pan. Don't worry if it gets crumpled: this will add to its rustic charm. Make one large incision in the centre to allow the steam to escape. Place the pan on a baking sheet to catch the drips, and then put it in the oven for 25 minutes or until the pastry is crisp and golden.

Remove from the oven and place a serving dish upside-down over the top of the pan. Invert both in one confident movement, allowing all the juices from the pan to arrive on the plate with the tart. Eat straight away, or later with lots of cream or crème fraîche.

✳ See note in the back about pastry volumes, page 273.

FOOD THAT KIDS LOVE
Serves four grown-ups and two children

Sugar-roast ham

This is the lunch that, summer or winter, we eat most often as a family down at Sam's. Ham is always much more delicious if home cooked. It is also a brilliant present for a new mum, so make an extra one at the same time (freeze the ham stock, too, for great soup and risotto). Serve with baked potato, Cheddar, salad (or crudités for kids), and whatever mustards, relishes and chutneys you've got in the back of the cupboard.

- 1 uncooked, unsmoked ham
- 2 tablespoons muscovado sugar
- 2 tablespoons runny honey
- 2 teaspoons English mustard powder
- black pepper

Weigh the ham to calculate the cooking time: it will need 20 minutes per 500g. Put it in a stockpot, cover with water and bring to a simmer, skimming off any scum that rises to the surface.

When cooked, drain the ham, reserving the stock to freeze for ham and pea soup. Preheat the oven to 220°C/gas 7. Cut off the net and slice off the rind of the ham, leaving the fat on. Score the fat in diamond shapes. Sit the ham in a small roasting tray, fat-side up.

Mix the rest of the ingredients into a paste – it should be quite solid and sludgy – and smear it over the ham. Bake for 30 minutes, basting halfway through. The ham should be a deep golden colour and a bit crispy – if not, put it under the grill for 5 minutes. Eat warm or cold.

Homemade pizza

Most fun is to make lots of small pizza, and buy a mixture of toppings: mozzarella, ham and mushrooms for kids to make their own, along with more sophisticated ones such as Roquefort, pine nuts, rocket, parma ham, and basil, to please the grown-ups, too.

for the dough
- 300g strong white flour, plus extra for dusting
- 100g rye flour (optional, but replace with strong white if not)
- 1 teaspoon fine salt
- 1 teaspoon fast-action dried yeast
- 350ml tepid water
- 5 tablespoons olive oil

for the toppings
- 150ml Lina's ragù (page 268), or passata
- 4 large balls mozzarella, thinly sliced (buffalo is a real grown-up treat)
- any combination of chopped ham, mushrooms, salami, olives, peppers, grated Cheddar, or whatever you'd like to sneak into your child's diet
- salt and black pepper

Make the dough as per the basic flatbread instructions on page 271, but replace a quarter of the strong white flour with rye flour for a slightly sour, chewier crust. Make in advance and allow to rise for 1–2 hours if you can, before knocking out the air and kneading again. If making the dough is a joint activity with kids, don't worry about the rise too much – it may not be quite as perfect but the eating and mess sacrifice will be worth the fun.

Preheat the oven to 230°C/gas 8, and if you have one, put a pizza stone in the oven to get hot. When the dough is ready, divide it equally into 12 balls about the size of a ping-pong ball. On a floured surface, roll out each ball as thinly as possible with quick, light motions.

Smear the pizzas with a little ragù or seasoned passata, then scatter over the mozzarella and whatever else takes your fancy – look for the different colours of olives and peppers if you want to make faces but don't expect the features to be eaten. Bake on the pizza stone or a flat baking sheet. You'll see them colour and puff to a perfectly chewy and crispy crust in 6–8 minutes.

Spaghetti with Lina's mini meatballs

Kids love anything small – mini carrots, peas, corn – unsurprising since everything else is proportionally twice the size to them. The trick to serving these successfully is to keep everything separate – toss the spaghetti with a little olive oil and put in one bowl, fry the meatballs and put in another, and have the tomato sauce in another too. That way no one can complain about bits they don't like.

- olive oil
- 600g spaghetti or favourite-shape pasta
- 800ml Lina's ragù (see page 268)

for the meatballs
- 250g minced beef or pork, or a mixture
- 75g fresh breadcrumbs
- 50g fresh ricotta

- 3 eggs
- 2–3 garlic cloves, finely minced
- small handful chopped parsley, preferably flat-leafed (leave this out if you have children who won't eat green bits)
- salt and black pepper

to serve
- Parmesan cheese, grated

Thoroughly mix all the meatball ingredients together in a large bowl until well combined. Dampen your hands and roll the mixture into 1cm balls (keeping your hands damp prevents the meat sticking to them).

About 20–30 minutes before you want to eat, heat 1cm of olive oil in a large, deep frying pan and fry the meatballs in a single layer, in batches if necessary, turning until they are golden all over – about 15 minutes per batch. Alternatively, you could grill them if preferred. Meanwhile, cook the pasta as per the packet instructions, and reheat the ragù in a saucepan.

Drain the pasta and toss it with a little olive oil to prevent it sticking. Serve the pasta, ragù, meatballs and grated cheese in separate bowls so everyone can choose which bits they wish to eat.

Crispy duck with pancakes

This is a very forgiving dish to cook – you can put it in the oven in the morning and simply leave it there until you want to eat it. Eat with rice and appropriate greens like pak choi, and don't forget to keep the soy sauce handy.

- 1 onion
- 1 orange
- 4 whole cloves
- 1 medium-large duck
- 2 tablespoons Chinese five-spice powder
- salt and black pepper

to serve
- 1 cucumber
- large bunch spring onions
- Chinese pancakes
- plum sauce

Preheat the oven to 150°C/gas 2. Halve the onion and orange, studding the orange with the cloves, and stuff them into the cavity of the duck. Prick the skin all over with a fork, then scatter with the Chinese five-spice powder and season very well.

Stand the duck on a wire rack over a large roasting tray – a huge amount of fat will render down which needs to drain off. Roast for 3¹/₂–4 hours, checking to see whether you need to discard the melted fat every so often.

Meanwhile, cut the cucumber into fine 8cm batons, and similarly shred the spring onions lengthways. When the duck is nearly ready, steam the pancakes in a bamboo steamer over a pot of boiling water according to the packet instructions.

Remove the cooked duck from the oven and pull it apart with two forks, shredding the meat with the grain away from the carcass. Eat as in a Chinese restaurant, spreading a spoonful of plum sauce over each pancake and adding pieces of duck, cucumber and spring onion before rolling up.

SOUP FOR UNEXPECTED VISITORS
Feeds four

Pea and blasted garlic soup

It is best to use fresh stock here, but Marigold granules will be fine if you're stuck.

- 1 whole bulb garlic
- 500g frozen peas or petit pois
- 500ml chicken or vegetable stock
- 1 generous dollop cream, crème fraîche or Greek yoghurt
- Parma or ready-cooked ham (optional)
- grated Parmesan (optional)
- salt and black pepper

Cut the top off the head of garlic so that the tips of the cloves are exposed. Blast in the microwave for 5 minutes until soft and mellowed. Squeeze out the cloves. Defrost the peas in the stock until the liquid is just coming to the boil. Add the garlic and season excellently.

Transfer the lot to a blender, adding the cream or whatever. Whiz until the soup is the desired consistency. Divide between bowls and shred a slice of Parma or regular ham over each, and a good grating of Parmesan.

Cucumber and yoghurt soup

It's best to make this soup in advance, so that the air bubbles can settle and it has time to chill properly. If you need to serve it immediately, though, add three or four ice cubes to the blender.

- 2 cucumbers, peeled, deseeded and roughly chopped
- 200ml Greek yoghurt
- 2 sprigs mint, roughly chopped
- 2 tablespoons cream
- sea salt and black pepper

Put all the ingredients into a blender, seasoning generously. Whiz until thoroughly combined and leave in the fridge to chill for up to 24 hours.

DRINKS FOR THE WEEKEND

Elderflower cordial

The appearance of elderflower marks the beginning of summer. Pick it on a sunny day, when it will be at its most fragrant. You will come across citric acid in old-fashioned chemists – stockpile it whenever you do, as it's quite rare to find. This recipe makes 2 litres.

- 1.5kg caster sugar
- 2 unwaxed lemons
- 30 elderflower heads
- 100g citric acid

Heat the sugar in a saucepan with 1.5 litres of water, stirring until it has completely dissolved, then bring to the boil. Slice the lemons and put them into a large bowl with the elderflower heads (shake them first to make sure there are no bugs).

Pour over the boiling liquid, stir in the citric acid, cover and leave at room temperature for 24 hours, picking out the lemon after a couple of hours. The next day, strain the cordial through muslin – or through an old (clean!) pair of tights – and store in a litre bottle with a top. It will stay good in the fridge for a few weeks.

Serve with fizzy water, ice, a couple of sprigs of mint and a slice of lemon for good measure. A shot of white rum will make it more interesting.

Bloody Mary

I don't know why this drink belongs so stolidly to weekends and plane flights, but it's worth knowing the classic recipe. If you have people who may prefer it alcohol-free, keep the booze aside and just add it to the glasses separately. Joe Gilmore, who was the head barman at the Savoy during the Second World War, and who I am very lucky to have as a neighbour, calls any version of a Bloody Mary without the vodka in a 'Bloody Shame'. Debate continues as to whether or not to drink this with ice, but I stand firmly with the Americans on this one.

- 4 celery sticks
- ice
- 300–400ml vodka
- 50ml cheap cream sherry
- 1 litre tomato juice
- juice of 3 lemons
- 1 teaspoon celery salt
- 5 tablespoons Worcestershire sauce
- 1 teaspoon Tabasco sauce

Halve the celery stalks and put one in each glass, along with plenty of ice. Shake the rest of the ingredients together well and divide between the glasses, or leave in a jug for people to help themselves.

Bullshot

Everyone remembers their first great love. Mine was for a city – New York – and I remember the exact moment I fell. I was 19, a stranger in the city, and was given the phone number of a devastatingly handsome friend of a friend. He invited me to his apartment and made me a bullshot. The tangy, savoury, icy concoction made me tingle all over. The taste of it will be forever connected to the rushing feeling of absolute joy. I didn't get to kiss him but I did get his recipe.

Variants of this classic drink include the Bloody Bull (exchange two parts of the consommé with two parts of Clamato juice), and Bloody Caesar (exchange all the consommé for Clamato juice).

- 2 parts vodka
- 4 parts Campbell's beef consommé (no other brand will do)
- 1 part lemon juice
- Worcestershire sauce, to taste
- Tabasco sauce, to taste
- ice

Shake the vodka, consommé, lemon juice, Worcestershire and Tabasco together very well and strain into a long glass over ice.

BASIC RECIPES AND OTHER
USEFUL INFORMATION

Some recipes are glamorous creatures that make the occasional appearance in your life, serving to intrigue and delight. Others are unshowy, but steadfast friends, either standing alone to form a simple meal, like pasta and her sauces, or existing as an important part of a more complex dish, like stocks and pastries. They are the roots of a cooking life that can grow in many directions.

The recipes that follow form the basis of so many dishes. They can all be frozen (apart from the pesto, which will keep in the fridge for weeks as long as it has a slick of olive oil over it) and it is worth making some of them in batches – like chicken stock and shortcrust pastry – as they will give you a head start on an impromptu occasion. Measure and mark the volumes when you label them – resealable plastic bags are extremely helpful for storing practically anything.

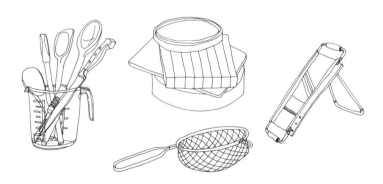

STOCKS
To make 1 litre

Fish stock

Fish stock is the main component in any fishy stew or soup. It's always worth adding discarded shells of shellfish as they impart particularly good flavours.

- 1 tablespoon olive oil
- 400g fish carcasses
- 150ml white wine
- 1 carrot, chopped
- 1 onion, chopped
- 1 celery stick, chopped
- 3 sprigs parsley
- 2 bay leaves
- sea salt

Warm the olive oil in a large saucepan. Add the fish carcasses, mixing and turning until any remaining scraps of flesh turn white. Deglaze the pan with the wine, scraping any sticky bits off the bottom, and let the alcohol bubble off. Add the carrot, onion and celery, herbs, a good scrunch of sea salt, and 1 litre of water.

Simmer gently for 45 minutes, skimming off any white scum that rises to the surface from time to time, then strain. You can freeze this, but label it clearly as you don't want to confuse it with other stocks.

Chicken stock

Chicken stock is the most useful of all stocks. I tend to stockpile chicken bones in the freezer until there's enough to be worth boiling up. The stock from a whole chicken is basically a broth fine enough to eat as soup (see page 145).

- 1 whole chicken, or 2 carcasses
- 2 fat carrots
- 2 celery sticks
- bunch parsley stalks
- 1 teaspoon black peppercorns
- 2 medium onions
- 2 bay leaves
- few thyme sprigs (optional)

Tuck all the ingredients as neatly as possible in a pan, breaking up the chicken carcasses so they take up as little space as possible. Cover with water – you'll need about 1.5 litres.

Bring to a simmer, skimming off any scum that collects on the surface. Once bubbles are just pricking the surface, partially cover the pan and allow it to prickle along at that speed for a couple of hours. If you are using a whole chicken, remove it after an hour, take off any meat you want to eat separately as it will be cooked, and return the bones to the pan.

When the stock has finished cooking, allow it to cool, then strain the stock and put it back into the stockpot. Bring it to the boil and reduce to the required strength or volume, then leave to cool.

Transfer to a container, cover and place in the fridge: the stock should turn into a light jelly and the fat will rise to the surface and solidify, making it easy to gently scrape off with a spoon and discard. Remember when you come to use the stock, it will want a fair amount of salt, particularly compared with a stock cube which is heavily salted to start with. You can freeze this, but label it clearly.

Vegetable stock

Vegetable stock can replace all other stocks for vegetarian versions of dishes. It's so quick to make it doesn't seem worth taking up the space in a freezer.

- 2 onions, diced
- 2 carrots, diced
- 1 leek, white part only, diced
- 2 celery sticks, diced
- 3–4 mushrooms, sliced

- bunch parsley stalks
- 1 thyme sprig
- 1 bay leaf
- 1 teaspoon black peppercorns

Put all the ingredients in a large saucepan with 1.5 litres of water and simmer, uncovered, for half an hour, skimming regularly. Strain and store.

Beef stock

I always buy fresh beef stock rather than make it. It's a complicated and long process best undertaken in professional kitchens.

THREE ESSENTIAL ITALIAN SAUCES
Feeds ten

Tomato ragù

Lina Malacrino, a wonderful Italian granny in Cardiff, taught me how to make this tomato sauce. The key to its richness is the extra olive oil, added as an ingredient rather than simply a base for frying. Lina doesn't believe you need to soften the onion first, and just bangs all the ingredients in together and leaves them to sort each other out, making it guilt-inducingly easy. However, you do need a food processor for this version; if you don't have one, chop the onions and fry them gently until softened first as per usual. Store the excess in the freezer.

• 6 x 400g tins peeled plum tomatoes
• 4 garlic cloves, peeled
• 1 large onion, roughly chopped
• 125ml olive oil
• handful shredded basil leaves
• 2 tablespoons sugar

• salt and black pepper

to serve
• small handful torn basil leaves
• grated Parmesan cheese

Combine all the sauce ingredients – apart from half the basil – in a large saucepan. Bring gently to the boil, then turn down to a simmer, partially cover the pan, and cook for 1–1¹/₂ hours.

Allow the sauce to cool a little, then blend it until smooth. Add the rest of the basil and allow the sauce to stand, overnight if possible. Reheat to serve, scattering over the final handful of basil and plenty of freshly grated Parmesan.

Meat ragù, or Bolognese if you will

The trick here is to give the meat a kick by the addition of some cured pork like smoked bacon, pancetta or chorizo. It gives the sauce a real zing and insulates it against blandness. It can be used successfully under mash as cottage pie, jammed into a baked potato, or just served with a green salad.

- 75ml olive oil
- 150g pancetta, cubed
- 3 medium onions, finely chopped
- 2 medium carrots, finely chopped
- 2 celery sticks, finely chopped
- 5 garlic cloves, squashed under the blade of a knife
- 1.5kg fairly lean minced beef

- 3 bay leaves
- small bunch thyme
- 1 x 400g tin chopped tomatoes
- 3 tablespoons tomato concentrate
- 500ml good beef or chicken stock
- $^1/_2$ bottle red wine
- salt and black pepper

Heat the olive oil in a saucepan large enough to take all the ingredients and fry the pancetta. When it colours, add the onion, carrot, celery and garlic, and fry for a further 5–10 minutes until they soften and begin to turn a little golden.

Add the mince, and fry on, breaking it up so that the meat can colour throughout. Then add the bay, thyme, tomatoes, tomato concentrate, stock and wine and bring to a simmer.

Turn the heat down, partially cover the pan and cook for 1–$1^1/_2$ hours. You'll need to check from time to time that it's not drying out.

When it's ready, pull out the thyme stalks (the leaves will have come off) and season to taste – I do like plenty of salt and pepper here. There may be a fatty slick on top that you can get with a spoon, though you'll want to leave some in, particularly if the sauce is to eat with pasta. If you want to temper it a little, you could add a dollop of crème fraîche or Greek yoghurt.

Classic pesto

Pesto is great for so much more than coating pasta. Fried up, it becomes an easy base to perk up quick-cooked everything: cold meat, boring veg. Mark, who is a tremendous pesto-maker, often uses other herbs instead of basil. Simply replace the basil with a combination of whatever herbs you like. If they are woody you need to carefully pick the leaves and chop them finely before pounding.

- 200g basil leaves
- 6 tablespoons pine nuts
- 4 garlic cloves, squashed under the blade of a knife
- pinch salt
- 200ml olive oil
- 120g pecorino or Parmesan cheese, finely grated

Pound together the basil, pine nuts, garlic and salt using a mortar and pestle, or whiz in a food processor. When they form a smooth paste, beat in the olive oil gradually in a steady stream. Finally, stir the cheese in by hand.

Pesto will keep in the fridge for a few weeks as long as you pour a slick of olive oil over the surface.

TWO TYPES OF BREAD
WORTH MAKING AT HOME

Homemade flatbread

If you've got an extra ten minutes, it's worth making this – people love eating bread straight out of the oven and are inevitably impressed by it. Once you're used to making it, there are plenty of extras you can knead into the dough: chopped sun-dried tomatoes, Parmesan, olives, rosemary – and anything else you can think of. This volume will make four pitta-sized breads.

- 200g strong white flour, plus extra for dusting
- $^1/_3$ teaspoon fast-action dried yeast
- $^1/_2$ teaspoon fine salt
- 170ml tepid water
- 2 tablespoons olive oil, plus extra for greasing

to garnish (optional)
- olive oil
- sesame seeds
- smoked paprika
- salt

Combine the flour, yeast and salt in a mixing bowl. Add the water and olive oil bit by bit, squidging it between your fingers.

Knead the dough firmly, stretching and massaging it for 5–10 minutes, until it becomes smooth and elastic. Set it aside in a bowl covered with a cloth to rise for at least 45 minutes – it can happily sit there all afternoon if needs be.

Shortly before you want to eat, preheat the oven to 230°C/gas 8.

Knock the air out of the dough by giving it another quick knead. Divide the dough into 4 balls and roll out into circles on a floured surface. You can smear a little extra olive oil and dust with salt, sesame seeds, or smoked paprika if you like.

Put the bread on a lightly oiled baking sheet and bake for 6–7 minutes – it will bubble up a bit and just begin to colour when it's ready.

Soda bread

Rory O'Connell, formerly head chef at the famous Ballymaloe cooking school in Cork, taught me to make this classic Irish bread. It is particularly good for Sunday mornings if you can't get – or can't be bothered to go for – fresh bread, and you can make one huge loaf by doubling the quantities (in which case, bake for an extra ten minutes). It is foolproof and quick, and you can experiment with a combination of different flours. Go for organic, stoneground flour if you can. Use a large, wide bowl for mixing the bread, as it will help keep more air in the dough.

- 285g brown wholemeal flour
- 285g plain white flour, plus extra for dusting
- 1 heaped teaspoon salt
- 1 heaped teaspoon bicarbonate of soda
- 425ml buttermilk or soured milk

Preheat the oven to 230°C/gas 8.

Mix together the dry ingredients in a large, wide bowl. Make a well in the centre and pour in most of the buttermilk or soured milk (the exact volume you will need will depend on how dry is the atmosphere in your kitchen).

Move your hand in a big circle, drawing flour from the sides into the wet middle of the bowl. If necessary, add more milk to make a dough that is soft, but not wet. It is not essential to knead this bread, and it's important not to overwork it.

Turn the dough out onto a well-floured surface, then wash and dry your hands. Fashion the dough into a round cake about 5cm high and place on a lightly floured baking sheet. Make a deep cross in the top of the bread and score each quarter lightly with a knife, to help it to rise.

Bake for 15 minutes, then reduce the oven temperature to 200°C/gas 6 and continue baking for a further 20–25 minutes. You'll know the bread is cooked if you tap the bottom and it sounds hollow. Leave it to cool on a wire rack.

PASTRY

Homemade pastry

I have to admit to using ready-made pastry in almost all situations. It's not that it's so hard to make – it's just that given the time available, it's rarely worth the effort. However, homemade pastry does bring that extra something to any pie or tart, and if you have a food processor, it becomes much easier.

Measuring volumes of pastry

When recipes refer to a quantity of pastry, such as 100g shortcrust pastry, what they are referring to is the weight of the flour in the pastry. So 100g shortcrust will be 100g flour, 50g butter, etc. Unfortunately, on pre-made packets, the weight refers to the entire weight of the finished pastry, so on these it would say 150g pastry. I have given both weights in the relevant recipes.

Working out how much to make

There is a rule that tells you how much pastry you will need but, annoyingly, you'll have to convert it from old-fashioned inches and ounces. It runs like this: subtract 2 from the inch diameter measurement of the flan ring to find out the weight needed. So, a 15cm/6in flan ring will want a 110g/4oz flour quantity of pastry, a 20cm/8in flan ring will want a 170g/6oz flour quantity of pastry, a 23cm/9in flan ring will want a 200g/7oz flour quantity of pastry, and so on. Phew.

Baking pastry

Pastry can either be baked in advance to make a pastry case (called 'blind baking'), or baked along with the rest of the dish. To blind bake, preheat the oven to 180°C/gas 4. Roll out your pastry, lay it into the tin and prick it with a fork. Line with parchment and weigh down with a couple of layers of dried beans. Bake for 15 minutes, remove the beans and paper and bake for a further 5–10 minutes until the pastry begins to turn golden. Allow to cool.

Shortcrust pastry

This is the most basic of pastries. It is made with twice the volume of flour to fat and bound with a little water. It is for savoury pies and tarts, although I don't mind using it in sweet baking as well, as I find it often offsets the sweetness of the fillings nicely.

- 120g plain white flour
- 60g chilled butter, cut into 1cm cubes
- pinch salt
- few tablespoons iced water

Sieve together the flour and the salt, and rub in the butter (or pulse in a whizzer) until the mixture resembles fine breadcrumbs. You want to work the flour as little as possible at all times to prevent the gluten developing, which makes it tough.

Add the iced water, tablespoon by tablespoon, until the mixture just balls together. Immediately wrap in clingfilm and chill in the fridge for at least 1 hour before rolling out and cooking as per recipe.

Rich sweet shortcrust pastry

This is the pastry to use for sweet tarts and pies. It is, as it says, rich, and if the filling is very sweet, you can often get away with using regular shortcrust instead.

- 120g plain white flour
- pinch salt
- 190g chilled butter, cut into 1cm cubes
- 140g icing sugar
- 1 egg yolk
- few teaspoons iced water

Sieve together the flour and salt. Rub in the butter (or pulse in a whizzer) until the mixture resembles fine breadcrumbs. You want to work the flour as little as possible at all times to prevent the gluten developing, which makes it tough.

Stir in the icing sugar and egg yolk, mixing gently until the pastry just comes together. You can add some iced water, teaspoon by teaspoon, if necessary. Immediately wrap in clingfilm and chill in the fridge for at least 1 hour before rolling out and cooking as per recipe.

Almond pastry

This crumbly pastry can be hard to roll out. I often make it into a fat sausage and cut slices off it to press into the tin. It works best as a base for soft fruit.

- 120g plain white flour
- 50g ground almonds
- pinch salt
- 90g unsalted butter, softened
- 50g caster sugar
- 1 egg yolk
- few drops almond essence

Sieve together the flour, ground almonds and salt. Rub in the butter (or pulse in a whizzer) until the mixture resembles fine breadcrumbs. You want to work the flour as little as possible at all times to prevent it from becoming tough.

Stir in the sugar, egg yolk and almond essence, mixing gently until the pastry just comes together. You can add a teaspoon or two of iced water if necessary. Immediately wrap in clingfilm and chill in the fridge for at least 1 hour before rolling out and cooking as per recipe.

Wine varieties and food matching

The information below should be taken very lightly, given that so many of the wines we drink are blends of different grape varieties. Listed here are some loose guidelines according to received wisdom:

Type:	Taste:	Food:
Pinot grigio	Crisp and dry, light	Easy-drinking and very light, it makes a great lunchtime wine
Riesling	Fruity with sweet hints	Sets off far-eastern spices, people either love it or hate it; I'm a fan, but prefer to drink it as an aperitif
Sauvignon blanc	Fruity but still dry	Currently the most fashionable white grape, works with difficult acidy foods
Viognier	Full-flavoured, fruity and floral	Low in acidity, this is a great alternative to Chardonnay and particularly good served with spicy foods
Chardonnay	Oaky and full-bodied	Was the wine of the nineties but there's been a backlash. It's the richest dry white; I love it and drink it with anything
Pinot noir	The lightest and fruitiest of reds	Good with game, poultry and fish. Served chilled, it is a wonderful summer red
Cabernet sauvignon	Deep rich red	The classic wine to accompany red meat, it is full-bodied and masculine
Merlot	Rich and a bit sweet	Not such a headache-inducer, goes with pinker foods like pork and tuna
Syrah/Shiraz	Rich with a bit of spice	Good with strong flavours like game, sausage, spicy rich food and cheese

My favourite flowers, and how to look after them

Whether it's an extravagant bunch or a tiny posy, there's no question that having flowers around the place and on the table brings a room alive. Here are some tips for how to look after the more obvious varieties.

Amaryllis: these huge winter flowers can last for a couple of weeks. Cut the stem on a slant – if the flowers look too heavy for the stem, you can insert a bamboo stick into the hollow centre. They look best by themselves in a tall vase.

Anemone: anemones are delicate and need lots of water. They will twist towards the light, and look lovely in multicoloured bunches, or mixed with similarly shaped flowers like ranunculus.

Chrysanthemum: don't turn your nose up at them – there are some really unusual and beautiful varieties, particularly the green ones. They are in bloom all year round, and can last for two weeks.

Dahlia: in season mid-summer to mid-autumn, they have come back into fashion and are great for splashes of rich colour at a brown and orange time of year.

Freesia: wonderfully scented, and great to sneak into mixed bunches for this reason. Look for plump buds with just one flower opening.

Gerbera: avoid touching the heads as they can damage easily. They are very sensitive to bacteria so clean the vase well and change the water often. As they age, their stems will bend into wonderful shapes, but you can keep them straight by winding fine wire carefully around them.

Hyacinth: hyacinths have the most wonderful scent and are great for infusing a room in deepest winter, when they are in season.

Hydrangea: these late summer flowers are unscented but their lovely large heads look wonderful clustered together. You can dry the reddish-brown autumnal blooms, which will look great for a couple of months.

Iris: hard to mix with other flowers as they are so sculptural – it's best to stick to long vases and just a few blooms.

Lily: look for plump buds with one flower just opening. They can last for a couple of weeks if you clip off dead flowers and leaves as they wither. Beware the red-brown stamen – it will stain anything it comes in contact with. Don't try to rub it off: instead, carefully remove with the sticky side of Sellotape.

Narcissus: cut the stems straight, and change the water often – their sap can kill other flowers quickly. The tiny white ones are highly scented, though the yellow daffodil is much more restrained. They tend to look best in generous bunches by themselves rather than mixed with other blooms.

Peony: unscented but to my mind the most beautiful of all blooms, especially when fully blown. Beware of tightly closed buds, particularly early in their season (May–June); they may never open at all.

Ranunculus: ranunculus look best at the end of their lives, when they are fully open and their petals turn almost translucent. Remove the lower leaves so that there are none under water level.

Rose: it's now thought that bashing stems damages their ability to drink, so cut them at a diagonal instead.

Sweet pea: sweet peas are very fragile and only last a few days. To refresh them, submerge completely in cold water for an hour, then shake them off, re-cut the stems and put them back in the vase.

Tulip: cut tulips straight across. They continue to grow after they are cut, and their stems will move and bend. To keep them straight, make a pin-prick through the stem just under the head.

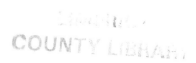

INDEX

Index

Index

ACKNOWLEDGEMENTS

Heartfelt thanks go to Tif Loehnis, the best agent-friend a person could ask for; to Rosemary Davidson for giving me the chance; to Richard Atkinson for picking up the baton with unswerving enthusiasm and bringing out the best in me; to Francesca Yorke, Clementine Hope and Georgia Vaux for making it look so beautiful; to Louise Candlish for the title; to Natalie Hunt and Jenni Muir for their patience and attention to detail; to Kate Bland for making noise; to Lisa Fiske for making it all run smoothly; and to everyone at Bloomsbury for their support and encouragement.

Thank you to Samantha Fletcher, Kate Weinberg and Daisy Garnett for being unnervingly mindful readers, editors, eaters, recipe-givers and testers, sisters, friends and generally brilliant people; to Sacha Bonsor and William Sitwell for giving me a break into food writing; to Jo Craven and Paddy Sutton for their garden; and to Cat Manson for rushing into the breech.

For their recipes, ideas, advice, testing and all other help, I'd like to thank Jess Avery, Nicholas Boles, Neil Chugani, Eve Claxton, Rory O'Connell, Taran Davies, Henry Dimbleby, Camilla Dinesen, Emma Dodson, Natasha Fairweather, Henry Faure Walker, Matt Fletcher, Rose Garnett, Joe Gilmore, Nixie Graham, Alice Haddon, Joff Heffer, Pev Hooper, Camilla and Julian Kingsland, Melinda Langlands-Pearse, Dom Loehnis, Leila McAlister, Henry McMicking, Lina Malacrino, Nigel Manson, Thomasina Miers, Claire Paterson, Demetra Pinsent, Natasha Richardson, Lilian Le Roith, Manuela da Silva, Laura Sinclair, Saskia Spender, Christian Spurrier, Lowri Story, Rick Strickland, Katherine and Cristian van Tienhoven, and everyone who let me practise on them.

Thank you to Dad, Noush and my whole family for supporting me, inspiring me, and feeding me so well.

And finally, Ed, my favourite and most long-suffering taster: thank you for believing in me, loving me, marrying me – and sometimes letting me work after supper, too.

And then ...

A NEW HOME, A NEW KITCHEN TABLE

The wonder of food, and cooking, is that you take it with you, wherever you go: a couple of rings in a student flat, a first cooker in the city, the kitchen of a holiday cottage. What's available to you in terms of kit and ingredients has an impact on what you make, but what your cooking life means to you, how you use it, remains the same.

So it was for me when I moved from east London to west. Amidst weeping and chocolate wrappers, Ed finally winkled me out of my old place. It took a good couple of months of self-pity before I emerged. And then, one crisp, early spring morning, I began to take notice of the new world on my doorstep.

My local shops are completely different now, crammed with Middle Eastern treasures like pale green sultanas, huge bags of pistachios and stacks of Turkish delight. In December, the streets will be piled with ruby pomegranate; in May, as I write this, they are paved with golden mangoes. The food on our table is likewise changing, taking on the fragrant tang of harissa, preserved lemon and quince. The one constant is that friends come round to share it with us.

It's a simple recipe for happiness, but for me it remains true: call a couple of friends over, bung a chicken in the oven, open a bottle of wine. Suddenly, you're at home.